D0195638

PRIVATE EYES:

A Writer's Guide
to Private Investigating

by
Hal Blythe
Charlie Sweet
John Landreth

Writer's
Digest
Books

Cincinnati, Ohio

Dedicated to Harold Blythe, Sr.; Luther E. Landreth; and Charles Sweet, Sr., three dads who started it all

Private Eyes: A Writer's Guide to Private Investigating. Copyright © 1993 by Hal Blythe, Charlie Sweet and John Landreth. Printed and bound in the United States of America. All rights reserved. No part of this book may be reproduced in any form or by any electronic or mechanical means including information storage and retrieval systems without permission in writing from the publisher, except by a reviewer, who may quote brief passages in a review. Published by Writer's Digest Books, an imprint of F&W Publications, Inc., 1507 Dana Avenue, Cincinnati, Ohio 45207. 1-800-289-0963. First edition.

97 96 95   5 4 3 2

Library of Congress Cataloging in Publication Data

Blythe, Hal
    Private eyes : a writer's guide to private investigating / by Hal Blythe, Charlie Sweet, and John Landreth.
        p. cm.
    Includes bibliographical references and index.
    ISBN 0-89879-549-4 (pbk.)
    1. Detective and mystery stories — Authorship. 2. Private investigators — Handbooks, manuals, etc. 3. Criminal investigation — Handbooks, manuals, etc.   I. Sweet, Charlie II. Landreth, John. III. Title.
    PN3377.5.D4B57   1993
    808.3'872-dc20   93-2890
                                                                                  CIP

Edited by Jack Heffron
Designed by Brian Roeth
Cover illustration by Chris Spollen

Acknowledgments

Special thanks to . . .

Marsha Blythe and Debbie Sweet, who were always there.
Lance and Chrisman, who are the best.
Ed Hino for a nick-of-time rescue.
Bill Tillett for his research assistance.
M.A.C.H.O. members Rick Givan, D.L. Richardson and Mason
    Smith for their constant encouragement, copious suggestions
    and meticulous editing.
Bill Brohaugh for his long-time faith in our abilities.
Jack Heffron for his editing and sensitivity.
The Richmond Police Department, State Police (Richmond Post),
    and Embry Curry, County Coroner, for their expertise.
Harry Moberly and Kenna Brandenburg for their research.
Debbie Busson and Devera Midgett for their clerical support.
The others (you know who you are).

About the Authors

Hal Blythe is a full professor at Eastern Kentucky University, where he specializes in creative writing. In addition to several hundred critical and pedagogical articles, he has co-authored numerous short stories with Charlie Sweet and is currently working on a novel, as well as another book for Writer's Digest.

Charlie Sweet is a full professor at Eastern Kentucky University. His specialty is American Literature. He has co-authored many articles and stories with Hal Blythe. Once a ghost writer for Brett Halliday's *Mike Shayne* series, he is currently collaborating on a novel, another Writer's Digest book, mystery weekends, and several articles with Hal Blythe.

John Landreth is a practicing private investigator in Richmond, Kentucky. An ex-policeman, he heads up the Special Operations Division for a local bank. He is currently writing a non-fiction account of some of his cases.

Photograph by Mark Kidd

Table of Contents

Studying the Interviewee
Closing the Interview

15 **Physical Evidence**   *123*

How to find pieces of the puzzle and put them to use in the investigation.

Types of Evidence
Following Up the Police Search
Collecting the Evidence
Putting the Pieces Together
Tainted or Manufactured Evidence

16 **Hired Help**   *135*

Turning to others for investigative assistance.

Basic Support
Expert Assistance
Contacts and Informants
Role-Players
Other Handy Helpers

17 **Making It Happen**   *143*

Acting as a catalyst helps stir the pot and gets the investigation cooking.

Stirring Things Up
Prodding the Suspect
The Honey Pot
Flamboyant and Simple Ruses

18 **The Report**   *150*

Putting the pieces together on paper after the investigation.

Goals of the Report
Building the Report Structure
Other Report Considerations
Billing the Client

"The PI's biggest advantage? They're like vampires. Nobody believes in them, and it's hard to do much to them."

—John Landreth

O N E

AN INTRODUCTION

I pulled the flame-red Ferrari in directly behind Louis Vee's parked car. His black, smoked-glass Caddy looked like a barbecue grill on wheels, and I felt ready to play backyard chef. Carefully I fitted the silencer over the barrel of my snub-nosed .38 Smith & Wesson Detective Special, then got out.

Tapping my gun on the driver's window, I flashed my gold PI shield. The glass dropped faster than a stripper's innocence.

"So what do you want, bub?" said the driver, Solly.

I yanked Louis's hired muscle through the window and pistol-whipped him so his nose leaked blood like oil from a teenager's hot rod. Louis took one look at the solitary cold eye of my S&W and began to sing like Madame Theodora's trained macaw.

Richard Steele,
Josh Shepherd, PI

Sound familiar? Like it could have been taken from a hard-boiled PI paperback? Maybe, but this excerpt from a fictitious novel illustrates one of the major problems with mystery and detective stories: The writer knows very little about how a real private investigator works.

While absolute fidelity to proper investigative procedure and the day-to-day routine is not necessary, probably not even desirable, effective writers need to create a sense of verisimilitude. After all, mystery readers expect an insider's view of the detective's world, and the quickest way to lose that audience's willing suspension of disbelief (not to mention an editor's interest in your manuscript) is to commit factual errors, display shoddy research, or generally portray PIs unrealistically.

The Need for Verisimilitude

A few years ago two of us were writing as Brett Halliday, ghosting the eponymous lead novella for *Mike Shayne Mystery Magazine.* Each month we were turning out 20,000 words about the adventures of America's longest continuously running private detective. Of the thirty-something stories we wrote, what do you think 90 percent of the readers who wrote letters to the editor were concerned about? Our near-perfect prose? Our intriguing labyrinthine plots? Our staccato, streetwise dialogue?

No. Verisimilitude. One reader from Spokane, Washington, pointed out that what we'd called a state-of-the-art sniperscope wasn't. A member of the Miami Police Department wrote that our Miami-based PI had in one tale violated proper chain of command to obtain information from the MPD. Another letter from Florida suggested that for working such dangerous cases around the Orange Bowl area, Shayne should double his fee.

Early on we learned our lesson about the illusion of truth. We contacted the MPD public relations division to obtain chain of command charts, publicity photos, maps of the city. We started reading the *Miami Herald* in our university library, and we wrote groups like the Miami Chamber of Commerce for any information we could get our hands on.

And when we started writing a series of books about A.E. Holliday, a Louisville-based detective, we decided we had to know more about how private investigators really work. We talked to the Jefferson County Police Department about their relationship with PIs. Research unearthed the Kentucky statute pertaining to the licensing of investigators. Then we struck up a relationship with John Landreth, a local PI with more than twenty years in the business. Our eyes were opened as John got down to the nitty-gritty about actual cases he had worked and legal ramifications in the field.

Debunking the Myths

John is an avid mystery reader; the duller the stakeout, the more avidly he reads. And, for the most part, what he finds in mystery fiction causes him to drop the book faster than a nonpaying client. One of his least favorite scenes is that seemingly obligatory moment where the cop/DA tells the PI to back off the investigation or, "I'll pull your ticket." In fact, most cops can't get an investigator's license suspended. States have regulatory divisions separate from local police to ascertain whether the detective has gone too far. In Ohio, for instance, the legislature has created a State Private Investigator

Advisory Commission. Another myth John dislikes centers on the bar where the detective is constantly swilling down the hard stuff in the midst of an investigation. To get much of anything accomplished, a PI has to be mentally and physically sharp, something precluded by volumes of alcohol. Many times when John has a drink in a bar while interviewing somebody, the glass is filled with ginger ale. In truth, the major beverage John consumes is coffee—always with three or more sugars. So much detective fiction is filled with gnats. Do you really think all PIs have offices with pebble-glass doors? Can every detective KO every opponent with one or two punches, then spend the next few days without so much as taking a single aspirin?

Mystery writers too often obtain the investigatory information they use from earlier PI novels. While some material is valid, quite often it is outdated, inappropriate for another locale, or simply wrong. Many myths get perpetuated and writers get lazy ("If it was good enough for Pulp Smith back in '57, it's good enough for me"). The best example of this myth perpetuation involves Dash Hammett. In *The Maltese Falcon* he describes a specific handgun, the Webley-Fosbery automatic revolver, as having a safety. This is one of the very few revolvers with a safety, and the gun itself even back then was extremely rare. But a generation later mystery writers still had their characters using such a collector's item, by then worth thousands of dollars. In addition, an awful lot of automatic revolvers in PI fiction (though not in real life) suddenly came equipped with safeties.

Our Goal

This book, then, is designed for you, the mystery writer, to get it right. Each chapter will treat a separate aspect of the investigator's world, progressing from obtaining a license to special problems. Each chapter will open with a passage from detective fiction, Richard Steele's *Josh Shepherd, PI*, then detail the reality, often emphasizing the gap between the popular concept and real life. Our ultimate goal is to provide sufficient details about an investigation so that you can respect your audience's intelligence and their desire for accuracy.

Why is a book such as this necessary? Look back at the passage from *Josh Shepherd, PI*. Richard Steele needs to do a little more research (as well as work on his prose style) if he wants to make

Shepherd's caper believable. Do you think a real detective would drive around in a billboard of a car like a "flame-red Ferrari"? A key to successful surveillance is invisibility, being able to blend into the environment. There's no such weapon as a snub-nosed .38 S&W Detective Special, and putting a silencer on a revolver is usually a study in futility. Furthermore, PIs are not exempt from civil or criminal codes. How many laws did Shepherd break by forcibly extracting Solly from the Caddy, pistol-whipping him, and intimidating his boss? Does Assault & Battery ring a bell? Then there's Shepherd's badge, his approaching the Caddy, his . . .

At the start we suggest that you ask yourself some key questions: Are you sure you want to write a PI novel? Do you really want to go to the effort to write a good one? Is your goal actually to write the Great American Novel, and you're taking the back door through detective fiction? If you are sincere, have a realistic assessment of detective fiction, and want to achieve the goal of fiction that John D. MacDonald said was "to tell it true," then read on.

Before starting, we offer some caveats. First, this book is intended as a guide, not a comprehensive treatise about detectives. Whole books have been written on some of our individual chapters. We offer a launch pad, not an entire universe. If you are interested in more detail, you can consult our "Works Cited and Secondary Sources" for additional information.

Second, our focus is mainly on the small-town PI, the one-person operation. Why? The majority of PI fiction is not written about Pinkertons or agents for large firms. In fact, the world's first fictional detective, C. Auguste Dupin, lived by himself and operated as a loner. While in real life the Burns and Wackenhut agencies have flourished, the fiction-reading public has remained fascinated with the rugged individual, that quintessential American prototype that mirrors our country's evolution in breaking away from traditional ties to seek a new path and new solutions on its own. Truthfully, too, major agencies often "farm out" investigative work to the small-towners.

A case in point. Back in 1967 when *Mannix* debuted on CBS, the gumshoe worked for Intertect, an investigative conglomerate run by computers and Lou Wickersham. The ratings weren't so hot, and the writers had difficulty coming up with inventive plots each week that pitted Joe Mannix against the corporate mentality. So when *Mannix* returned for its second year, the detective operated a one-man shop aided only by his secretary.

Besides, reality being what it is, the expert in the writing of this book is John, who has spent the majority of his investigative career as a small-town PI.

Third, we are not advocating turning your stories into encyclopedias on detectives. A major part of the police procedural's appeal is the illusion of voluminous inside information; with PI fiction, a little information goes a long way, but it must be accurate.

Fourth, we will try to tell the truth about PIs, not paint a portrait of a modern-day white knight. But, truthfully, this goal presents some problems. There is no national, must-join organization of PIs that acts as a clearinghouse for information or even surveys its own membership. In preparing this book we sent out questionnaires to every national organization of PIs. We had a net total of zero responses. Secrecy is the trademark of the profession; clients don't want information about them divulged, and individual PIs don't like to aid the competition by revealing tricks of the trade. Also, the detective biz is a transient profession; people drift in and out of it on a daily basis. As a result, little data, especially recent, exists, and much of the data that can be found is "tainted" because researchers usually lump apples — PIs — with oranges — private security agencies.

An Invitation

"Down these mean streets a man must go," wrote Raymond Chandler, but the creator of Phillip Marlowe didn't mean that the eyes of the writer or the detective should be closed. Join the three of us as we show you how to shine the spotlight of authority on those mean streets and guide you from getting into the business and setting up shop to closing the case file.

JOB REQUIREMENTS

So what if Louis Vee had more juice than the nuclear reactor on Three-Mile Island and more soldiers in his organization than the Red Army? I wasn't about to back down. I was in my prime — 6 feet 4 inches, 220 pounds, and I spent more time in Gold's Gym than Gold himself. And seven years on the city police force had taught me a lot of ways to scrape bugs like Louis Vee off my windshield.

Richard Steele,
Josh Shepherd, PI

This cliché of the physical ex-cop turned PI has appeared so often in print and film that some writers have come to think it's the only possible background for a detective. Stats show that back in 1985 more than 40,000 licensed detectives were working in this country, so it stands to reason that PIs come in all sizes and from all walks of life. Though a lot are ex-cops, thousands of paths into the profession exist, and writers can choose to follow the less-traveled roads.

Previous Experience

John actually began his law enforcement career as an assistant manager for a local branch of CIT, a large New York-based finance company. Despite the title, most of his job entailed repossession work and tracing "skips" who stopped paying back loans. After a stint as an intelligence officer in the Army, he joined the police force of Lexington, Kentucky. Then to help finance his college education he became a county probation officer in Estill County, Kentucky.

That led to PI work for a bonding company and eventually a job with a local judge's detective agency. He is currently Chief of the Special Operations Division of a bank. In addition to his wide background in law enforcement, he has a B.A. from Eastern Kentucky University in Speech and Drama. Not only has his acting ability helped him with role-playing in many cases, but as a sidelight it got him some small parts in movies. In fact, if you want to know what John looks like, check out the villain in *The Thoroughbreds*.

A West Coast gumshoe, Josiah Thompson, has been in the business for fifteen years. Before that, he was a professor of philosophy at Haverford College in Pennsylvania. While on a sabbatical in San Francisco to research a book on Nietzsche, he developed writer's block and a bad marriage. On a whim he decided to be like one of his favorite literary characters, Walter Mitty, and applied for a job in a Bay Area detective agency. Recently Thompson published a book, *Gumshoe*, about his personal odyssey from being a privileged child to an adult PI.

William Callahan is president of United Intelligence, Inc., a large firm with an office on New York's Park Avenue and yearly revenues in excess of $1 million. Callahan, who sounds like a model for Clint Eastwood's Dirty Harry, began as a law student at St. John's University. After clerking for former President Richard Nixon's law firm, he joined the Justice Department.

Edmund Pankau heads up Intertect Inc., the largest detective agency in Texas. Although he now has thirty investigators working for him, Pankau started by himself as an IRS agent in Florida. On his way to another law enforcement job in Oregon, he got stuck in a rare Houston snowstorm. The snow melted, and he's still there.

Dan Eisenberg, founder and first president of Miami's Tracers Company of America, really entered the business in his childhood. After unsuccessfully trying to locate two rich uncles, Eisenberg was asked by a neighbor to find her long-lost brother. The stock market crash in 1929 provided him with a huge list of clientele as so many people ran from their financial obligations.

Emmanuel C. (Mike) Ackerman was Phi Beta Kappa at Dartmouth when he joined the CIA. An eleven-year stint with "The Company" ended with his leaving after congressional meddling in the agency. He and a retired agent opened their own firm, The Ackerman Group, a security business with $3.5 million in revenues and a specialty in hostage negotiations.

Other investigators did take a more traditional route. Ed Hino, who operates his own agency outside of Philadelphia, is a retired agent from the FBI. In fact, his business card announces he is a member of the Society of Former Special Agents of the Federal Bureau of Investigation. Florence Sperbeck, an Oakland detective with more than 10,000 cases under her belt, started as a police clerk there. Jerry Bussard, who runs the AAA Detective Agency in Kenwood, Ohio, left the Columbus police force after fifteen years to become a private detective. Jim Simmons was a Marine surveillance expert in Vietnam who used radar and electronics to track Viet Cong movements. He now operates Security American Protection Services Inc. in Northside, Ohio.

In short, a PI rarely enters the field without some sort of law enforcement background. No matter how strong your detective's motives, without some training in the field, the detective comes across as unrealistic. Attitude without aptitude is insufficient. In real life, most of us don't jump into a lake until we've stuck our toe in or checked the water's depth.

Getting Physical

Do size, gender and age matter? Does every detective have to be an over-six-foot hulk like Robert Parker's Spenser, an ex-boxer, who in a recent novel tied one hand behind his back and still managed to pummel a pack of Neanderthal thugs?

In real life, size and age vary. Ed Hino, who lives in a Philly suburb, is 5 feet 10 inches, 180 pounds, about the same size as when he played quarterback for George Washington University. Mike Ackerman is over fifty years old and stands 5 feet 10 inches. Dan Eisenberg is in his seventies, as is Florence Sperbeck. The S & Elle Detective Agency near London, England, is run by two women in their late thirties. Jay J. Armes, an El Paso investigator, lost both hands in an accident when he was a teenager. W. Russel Gray once studied Philadelphia-based single operative offices and determined the average height of these real detectives was 5 feet 10 inches; the average weight, 175 pounds.

In the past 150 years, fiction writers have created two opposite detective stereotypes. On one hand, the PI is portrayed as Sam Spade, a tough but tarnished knight on a moral quest to right wrongs primarily with his fists and his .38. On the other is the Nero Wolfe type who sends his legmen out to do the physical work, then sits back, cogitates and brilliantly solves crimes through the genius of his tiny gray cells.

In real life most investigators fall somewhere in between. John, who by the way is 5 feet 10 inches and 185 pounds, admits there have been situations where he's used his fists and an arsenal that rivals the National Guard's. Sometimes, though rarely, he's solved cases without leaving his office by simply using his three favorite operatives—his brain, his telephone and his long list of contacts.

One such case involved a couple who asked him to check their son's financial condition. The son, who was a sergeant in the U.S. Army, kept writing to ask them to send him money supposedly to help pay for his daughters' operations. Right off, John figured the son was lying about the medical expenses if not the operations themselves. Having been in the Army himself, John knew that as a government dependent, the son and his family were provided full medical care by the government. Obviously the son was making up hardship stories to bilk his parents, who didn't want to turn down their only child. A few calls revealed the money was financing some rodeo horses, some tack and some gambling.

Dan Eisenberg has traced many people by relying on his vast collection of telephone books. Sally Denton and Bonnie Goldstein, two Washington, D.C.-based investigators, prefer to read over public documents and locate on-the-record interviews. Likewise, Ed Pankau likes the telephone. If the missing person in question is a secretary, he calls a notary public board; a bowler, he dials the American Bowling Congress. Real-life PIs try to join as many lodges as possible (anything for a brother Elk, Moose, Bison, etc.).

But most searching is physically oriented. Mike Ackerman once chartered a helicopter to fly over northern Guatemala to personally pay a half-million dollar ransom. Josiah Thompson, though he refuses to carry a gun, flew to India to rescue a child kidnapped by his father. John believes that 95 percent of his time is taken up driving his car around to various interviews. To him, the phoniest TV detective ever was David Janssen as Harry O., who in the first year of the show had no car and had to make do with public transportation. A PI needs a car. John figures that an average out-of-state case will take five days during which he will put around 1,200 miles on a rental vehicle.

Having the Personality for It

No matter the type, is there a necessary personality trait that makes a good detective? According to Irwin Blye (a PI for more than thirty years who has worked some 15,000 cases and written a book, *Secrets of a Private Eye*), PIs are sort of like Boy Scouts: They must be diligent, observant, prepared, resourceful, creative, inquisitive, patient and neutral. In his *Practical Guide for Private Investigators*, Edward Smith reduces the list to four necessary traits: objectivity, thoroughness, reliance, accuracy.

Persistence stands out. A PI must be willing to tail a suspect for days as well as pore over courthouse records in a musty vault for long hours. For fictional PIs, the first trail they follow usually pays off; in real life it's try and try again. William Callahan spent more than nine months on one case tracking down the Shah of Iran's personal assets. John recalls a case that necessitated more than twenty trips from Kentucky to the West Coast from March to October. Was it worth it? In the end, he found the missing child alive and returned him. Moreover, he's found the emotional high from such successes can carry him through months of routinely dull cases.

Aggressiveness is another vital skill. John thinks of himself primarily as a catalyst. "Sooner or later you've collected all the information you're going to get, and you're still stumped. The only way to break the case is to make something happen." Investigators have to be willing to keep knocking on doors, to refuse to take no for an answer, to go where they aren't wanted, and to mix with socially unacceptable people — things the average citizen doesn't want to do. It isn't always what the detective does; it's often how or what his pressure in the case causes others to do.

And PIs have to be curious — they've got to know why, who, where or when. Once, on a missing person case, John's client got a phone call on the anniversary of the date her husband had disappeared, saying the husband was alive. The woman hit her Caller I.D. button. John traced the number to a phone booth outside the Continental Inn in Lexington. John had learned earlier that his client's missing husband had left her and lived with another woman, whose previous boyfriend was a musician. On the anniversary of the call, John discovered the boyfriend had been playing — you guessed it — the Continental Inn. The time of the call? During a musician's break. Question, John asked himself: How had the musician known the date the husband had disappeared unless he had had something to do with the disappearance?

John believes in healthy paranoia. He's learned to be skeptical when he puts his car in the shop. When he gets it back, he checks to see that nothing has been added or deleted. He worried when he was younger that the kids' baby-sitters might be paid to look through his files. In motel rooms, he sticks ashtrays in the coats he leaves in suitcases (if the case is opened, the ashtray moves). And he constantly wonders if local and federal authorities might try to set him up with prostitutes or drugs.

Rotten Apples

In PI fiction, detectives may be recovering alcoholics, ex-cops who were booted off the force, disgraced war heroes, Neanderthals quick with their fists, or aloof aristocrats who occasionally condescend to help the great unwashed. But they are still knights in slightly tarnished armor.

In real life, the PI is not always a knight or even a squire, but often a knave. John estimates that of all the PIs he's encountered, at least half are in the business for less than honorable reasons — sex, ego, quick money earned by exploiting the innocent and the vulnerable. He calls these PIs "rotten apples." Common types include the Cowboy, the Staller, the Turncoat and the Mine-Salter, all of whom you will meet in sidebars placed throughout the book.

Though many of these rotten apples have been caught employing their unscrupulous methods, they continue to operate, preying on their clients for all they can get. The very nature of PI work lends itself to abuses. Face it. If the detective doesn't have much work and is getting paid by the day for a case, what is the incentive to provide an immediate solution?

PIs who break the law are still private citizens and *can* be subjected to civil suits. However, because PIs know so much about their clients, the clients tend not to raise allegations of wrongdoing. For this reason, licenses are difficult to revoke.

Obtaining a License

Size, age, gender, physical ability, background — none of these things seems to matter when you set out to create a private eye. As long as your detective has one or more of the personality traits, you're ready to go.

But there are some restrictions. The most important limitation involves exactly where you want your detective to set up shop. Each state has different requirements, different definitions of the PI, and there are a number of variables:

- minimum age (e.g., California is 18; Arkansas, 25)
- residency (both the particular state and the U.S.)
- character (usually "good moral . . ." is specified)
- written exam
- criminal record (many states exclude convicted felons)
- previous related experience (e.g., in Arizona three years as a police officer or one year as security guard; in Maryland three years as police investigator, five years as a full-time licensed investigator, or ten years as a police officer)
- insurance (e.g., liability in Iowa)
- surety bond (e.g., $2,000 in Wisconsin; $25,000 in Vermont).

Interestingly, some states such as Kentucky, Virginia, Oregon, South Dakota and Oklahoma have no regulations on the detective industry. Other states put restrictions on investigators for revenue purposes only.

Since the laws governing private investigators are particular for each state and are quite often complex, you must take time to research the specific statutes under which your detective will work. A few likely sources:

- Libraries. Most public libraries have copies of the statutes; almost all college libraries do, as do many lawyers' libraries.
- State attorney general's office.
- Local police station.
- Local attorneys.
- State regulatory agency. This agency is often affiliated with the state's departments of public safety, licensing or police.

For a list of these agencies, consult the latest edition of Cunningham and Taylor's *Private Security in America* (Boston: Butterworth-Heineman). The following states, however, do not have an agency regulating the security industry:

Alabama	Oklahoma
Colorado	Oregon
Idaho	Pennsylvania
Kansas	Rhode Island
Kentucky	South Dakota
Louisiana	Tennessee
Mississippi	Washington
Missouri	Wyoming
Nebraska	

Get It Right

As we suggested earlier, verisimilitude in fiction refers in general to a work's semblance of reality. More exactly, the technique usually involves the writer providing abundant, specific and correct details to create the illusion of reality for the reader. So, if your story reveals your Little Rock-based PI has just received a B.S. in criminology on his twenty-third birthday and has opened an office, you've started on the wrong foot. Maybe your readers won't notice or know Arkansas law, but, more important, this mistake could domino throughout your manuscript by destroying your basic credibility.

Your best tack, then, is to begin with as much realistic detail as possible. Readers realize quickly that if they catch one mistake early, there are bound to be more later on. When you start to fill out a bio on your PI protagonist, take the time and make the effort to get it right. Start by researching your chosen state's laws governing the detective industry.

Say you'd like to write a story about a PI who operates out of the retirement community of Venice, Florida, and for nostalgia's sake you want to set the tale back a decade. How do you achieve verisimilitude? You start by getting hold of the *Florida Statutes* from around ten years ago. In the 1983 volume (one Hal and Charlie grew acquainted with when they started the *Mike Shayne* series), chapter 493 takes ten pages of small print to spell out INVESTIGATIVE AND PATROL SERVICES; DECEPTION DETECTION. This chapter lists nine distinct classes of licenses, each with different requirements. Does the class matter? Absolutely. If you give your detective a Class A license, s/he can't carry a firearm. Moreover, a Class B licensee cannot investigate crimes, only guard. Liability insurance? Your detective must carry $300,000's worth in most cases. And make sure your PI posts the license in "a conspicuous place" where a client can see it. A Class G detective? Your PI must then have a statewide firearms permit and carry only "a standard police .38 revolver."

In Pennsylvania, prospective PIs must file an affidavit listing several people who know them (two persons must be in law enforcement and attest to the applicant's efforts in that field). Then the applicant must attend a hearing in which both the judge and a representative of the district attorney's office ask him/her questions. Gun permits in the Quaker State are a separate matter, and applications are made to the local sheriff.

Obviously, then, each state, each class has different requirements/prerequisites. Knowing your state's laws can also help you create a more realistic plot. For instance, if a detective solves the crime by posing as a state policeman, Florida authorities will take disciplinary action involving a possible fine, reprimand or revocation of license. Likewise, Florida law prohibits the PI from the commission of "assault, battery and kidnapping" in a case. Being conscious of these restrictions allows you to be believable while forcing you to devise ingenious ways to get around them.

10 Tips 4 Interviewing Authorities

Throughout this book we stress that to obtain some basic information (e.g., laws governing local PIs, license plate numbers) you need to talk to the relevant authorities. Ideally, you should set up interviews ahead of time, but even if you just drop in on your experts, here are some hints about the best ways to approach them.

Go early. In researching this book we tried all different times to see people. We found that the hour to strike is when they first arrive at work. They're fresh, they haven't got their daily routine started, they haven't had to put up with a day of crank calls and obnoxious people, and their computers, not yet up, haven't had time to go down.

Dress respectfully. While coat and tie or dress is not necessary in most cases, a clean, casual outfit sets a proper tone. Of course, grooming should be considered since you want to appear as a professional commanding respect. You also want to put the officials you talk with at ease—you want them to chat honestly, not to hold back information or to tell you what they think you want to hear.

Identify yourself. Clearly give your name and mention your credentials—doctor, lawyer, freelance writer.

Explain your purpose immediately. Tell them exactly what you want and why (e.g., writing a book, intense desire to be a PI). Most people on hearing you're writing a book are flattered; secretly they'd like to have their name and views in print.

Display a good attitude. Show them and their profession respect. Don't be overbearing ("I'm the taxpaying investigative journalist, and you're the public official whose job is to give me, your real employer, what I want"). Don't be deadly serious or a comedian in training. Public officials today are publicity conscious and realize the value of good public relations.

Try to avoid distracting, frightening paraphernalia. Tape recorders and even copious notetaking put people off. If you don't think you can remember what you're told, try using a small, unobtrusive recorder (and get their permission to tape).

Prepare a list of specific questions in advance. Working people can't spend a lot of time just shooting the breeze. People trained in a specific area are used to dealing with precise information in that area. They respond better to "How can I obtain the XYZ Form?" than "What do you know about motor vehicles?" Keep your list of questions brief. People are donating their time, and you can always come back.

Listen. You're there to obtain information, not to dazzle the official with your expertise.

Close cordially. Thank the person and leave a card.

Take notes as soon as the interview is over. While both the interview and the interviewee are fresh in your mind, jot down recollections.

Summary

As you can see, state regulations can be quite specific, and while you may never use every relevant statute you discover, you should be aware of them. Most writers spend a lot of time researching the plot; for example, for a story involving heart attacks, research into the new biotechnical tp-a's (a gene-spliced agent that dissolves blood clots in the heart) would be mandatory. But consider that since your story (and perhaps future stories) most likely begins and ends with your detective, the most important information you obtain is that which relates to the creation of your detective.

Hints

1. If you would like to talk with a real detective in your area, consult the Yellow Pages under DETECTIVES/PRIVATE INVESTIGATORS.

2. If you desire the name of a PI in Paris, *The Regency International Directory*, published in England, lists investigators around the globe, providing their specialty (PD is their code for private detectives), names and addresses. The RID is actually a multivolume compilation of other directories.

3. If you want to know if there's a detective in Dubuque, *The Security Letter SourceBook* (printed annually) has a chapter devoted to national agencies (including their specialties) as well as a list of local investigators (organized by state, then city). Published annually, too, the *Time Finance Adjusters* (call 1-800-874-0510) contains a state-by-state, city-by-city listing (and some pictures) of selected bonded skip tracers, recovery agents, professional adjusters and loss consultants.

Types of Practices

With the info Louis Vee had so graciously volunteered, I headed back to my office. One block away from urban renewal, the MacDonald Building was home to a lot of seedy characters — panhandling winos, a one-legged prostitute, some numbers runners, a penny-ante crack dealer who couldn't afford reinforced walls, and me. Kicking the green and brown bottles off the sagging stairs, I headed up to the third floor room that held The Josh Shepherd Agency. That was me. I worked by myself and I liked it that way.

Richard Steele,
Josh Shepherd, PI

Once again Richard Steele has found it easy to lapse into a time-honored tradition in detective fiction — the PI prowls those mean streets *alone*. A closer look at some of the great literary lone wolves reveals the one-person operation isn't always quite that. Sherlock Holmes used a competent physician for a legman. C. Auguste Dupin had an unnamed aide-de-camp. Sam Spade started with Miles Archer. And even the super sleuth of Beantown, Spenser, has a predatory sidekick named Hawk. In real life the term private eye comes from the advertising slogan "The eye that never sleeps" for the famed Pinkerton Detective Agency — the Pinkertons.

Although many writers get wrapped up in the great American myth of the rugged individual and its detective version, the solitary PI types of agencies are as variable as the imaginations of the owners. Every PI does not set up shop in a big city, and every PI, as Sue Grafton, Sara Paretsky (and Agatha Christie before them) have demonstrated, need not be male.

How broad is the field? Statistics are almost impossible to obtain. First, the nature of the business is secretive. Membership in any kind of national, state or local organization is not mandatory or productive. People enter and exit the business rapidly. Since some states have virtually no regulations, a person could be a cop one day, a PI the next, and a used-car salesman the third. How do you tell part-timers from full practitioners?

California PI Sam Brown thinks there are about 65,000 investigators in this country. *Entrepreneur Magazine* reported in 1988 that the average agency made from $75,000 to $100,000 annually. According to a Hallcrest Systems' 1981 survey of private investigators, the average agency had three full-time employees, one part-timer, and brought in gross annual revenues somewhere between $50,000 and $100,000.

One-Person Operations

This is really a misnomer. Most PIs who go into business by themselves have some type of support/part-time help — secretary, accountant, specialists/consultants for specific jobs, freelancers. Unassisted one-person agencies are rare, but they do exist.

For instance, Marilyn Greene, a woman who has co-written (with Gary Provost) a book, *Finder*, about her experiences, operates by herself out of Schenectady, New York. She tends to use common-sense elementary investigative techniques, personal research and her own book collection. She even types her own case files, which she keeps in her basement office.

Ed Hino operates out of his home in Lansdale, Pennsylvania. A full-time law enforcement instructor and department head at a nearby community college, Hino is supported by a computer, an accountant and two part-time investigators.

For the most part John has also been a loner. Why? He claims nobody is crazy enough to go along with him — unless he counts the volunteers who want to learn the trade firsthand. His is still the sole name on the business card. The only thing that's changed over the years is his address. Currently his office is located on the second floor of a bank on Main Street, Richmond, Kentucky. His office is run so un-officelike that the box of letterhead stationery he bought in 1976 still has twenty or so sheets left.

One-person operations, especially those in small towns and when a PI is getting started, tend to be like general practitioners.

To put bread on the table, to develop a client base, and to build up goodwill, they have neither the luxury of specializing nor of picking and choosing their cases. But circumstances intervene to push PIs into a specialty. Marilyn Greene, for instance, has become a modern-day, real-life version of the old radio show Mr. Keen, Tracer of Lost Persons. Over the years she has gotten results in finding lost persons. Because of the resulting publicity, clients now tend to seek her out. In fiction, Andrew Vaach's detective, Burke, deals primarily with children, especially abused ones, and Spenser seems to prefer the trendy cases dealing with kidnapped children/lesbians, blackmailed politicians/athletes and child prostitutes.

Small Agencies

Just as writers collaborate, so do detectives. This type of agency has a minimum of two people but fewer than a small corporation.

Goldstein & Denton of Washington, D.C., is a two-person PI agency — Sally Denton and Bonnie Goldstein. Since they work in a big city, they tend to be white-collar sleuths, working primarily for corporations researching personnel.

William Callahan's Unitel has grown bigger as he has become more well known. By 1989 he employed fifteen operatives. Using former law enforcement officers, Callahan has made a reputation with white-collar crime and in his words is becoming "much more international" with interests in worldwide terrorism and takeovers.

Intertect Inc., the largest agency in Texas, has more than thirty investigators. Operating out of Houston, it not surprisingly works on S&L scams by tracking down con artists and seizing their assets. Appropriately, Ed Pankau's outfit is located in a top-floor office of a building acquired from a failed S&L.

Corporations

As our country's economy has become progressively global and white-collar crime has grown, it's no wonder that large detective corporations have developed, leaving divorce cases and their like to the smaller shops. Of course, large agencies such as the Pinkertons have been around for more than a century.

In 1850 Allen Pinkerton, who invented the term "operative"

because "detective" had become associated with graft, founded the Pinkerton National Police Agency aka Pinkerton's National Detective Agency in Chicago. Beginning as private bounty hunters used to guard the railroads and express companies, Pinkerton expanded his company into a worldwide agency complete with uniformed night watchmen (The Pinkerton Protective Patrol), which was a national police force (though private) before the FBI.

National Guardian is a nationwide company that specializes in home-protection units and guards.

Jules Kroll heads up the New York City-based Kroll and Associates. Employing around 200 people, the firm enjoyed 1989 revenues of about $50 million. A fifth of its work is devoted to researching mergers and acquisitions. They check into the backgrounds of companies as well as the people who head them.

Summary

John says that over the years many people have approached him wanting to learn the trade. Most were willing to serve an apprenticeship, work for free, or in some cases to pay John just to work for him. A few of these offers have been accepted for a while, and a couple of people even turned out to be good at the trade. But even they did not stay very long. All and all, John says, "It's a very rough racket. Physically, emotionally and financially. As one ex-cop turned PI out of Louisville said a year or two ago, 'In this business, it's chicken one day and feathers the next.' "

Hints

1. If you want to discover how a PI really works, whether as a one-person op or a multistaffed shop, you'll probably have to visit. PIs are notoriously poor about giving information over the phone or answering unsolicited queries about their business.
2. If you're interested in the workings and formations of larger agencies, you could check out William Hunt's *Front-Page Detective* (Bowling Green: Popular Press, 1990) on William J. Burns and the Burns Agency.

AREAS OF SPECIALIZATION

*I paused in front of the frosted-glass door that had my signature on it.
I looked forward to entering the same way I anticipated that pair of root
canals Doc Tudor had scheduled for me next week. My desk was littered
with more files than an IRS office, and my answering machine had
probably run out of tape. Where to start? Skip-trace for Shylock
Bartholomew? That repo for River City Insurance? Finding the hot
paper Funderburk had taken from Clark & Associates? Answering
Judge Brack's zinger? Spelunking in the courthouse vault? Prying the
Caputo kid loose from that chicken farm? Tailing a wandering John for
H.M. Pulliam, Esq.? Then there was the Rideout homicide . . .*

Richard Steele,
Josh Shepherd, PI

Yes, loners like Josh Shepherd, whether their goal is truth, justice,
the American way, or putting bread on the table, work more than
one case at once, and they often play catch-as-catch-can. Still, small
shops, like large corporations, tend to do one thing better than others, and because they do, they develop a reputation that serves as a
magnet for clients needing their specialty. But, almost never does a
PI work a murder investigation. That job is left to professional police
forces. In rare cases, a PI might be retained by a civilian after an
initial homicide investigation has borne little fruit.

From a practical standpoint, you as a writer can't possibly know
enough about all the various fields detectives really investigate.
Therefore, it's probably in your best interest to have your PI investigate crimes in areas in which you have 1) the expertise, 2) an interest, and/or 3) access to necessary information.

In truth, real PIs work in a lot more fields than most fiction
gives them credit for. Here are some to consider.

Missing Persons

Actually, this field is so large that it has almost as many subcategories as there are other areas of specialization. Milk cartons and lurid TV tabloid shows aside, the truth is that most missing people are missing because they want to be. People disappear essentially to escape unpleasant realities—the inability to live with parents, spousal incompatibility, financial problems (whether they take the money and run or they run because they can't pay), thwarted romances and psychological problems. Occasionally people do disappear against their will (such as being involved in a crime like kidnapping or homicide), but this circumstance is rare.

The major distinction in missing person cases is the age of the missing person. Children, because of their inherent helplessness, create an urgency in the need to locate them. However, almost all missing children show up immediately; they've simply wandered off at the mall or gone down the street to visit another child. In 95 percent of the remaining cases, the child has been taken by a non-custodial parent/relative without the custodial parent's permission, and most of these cases are criminal matters handled by the police (as are the other 5 percent). Teenagers (from adolescence to twenty-one), usually considered missing after they've been gone for twenty-four hours, are missing for the most part because they want to be. They've run away to escape a problem that's become too large for them to handle. Likewise, adults, declared missing after twenty-four to seventy-two hours (varying from state to state), are for the most part voluntarily missing.

Three Books Every PI Writer Should Have

1. Ferraro, Eugene. *You Can Find Anyone!*, Santa Ana, California: Marathon Press, 1988. This comprehensive book provides numerous sources to help a PI locate most people. Included are differing directories (telephone, cross-street and city) plus addresses, Armed Forces offices, state-by-state listing of agencies to write for vital statistics (birth, death, marriage and divorce certificates) and driving records (title, registration, accident reports), Social Security offices, phone company numbers (as well as scams to get inside). Ferraro also notes the various groups that work with runaway children and adoption agen-

cies. Even clip services and outside help (e.g., vehicle operator searches, Executive Search Corp.) are mentioned, and a Post Office Search Request form is described.

2. Berko, Robert, and Sherry Sadler. *Where to Write for Vital Records*, Orange, New Jersey: Consumer Education Research, 1989. Sometimes the two texts overlap. This book also lists state-by-state sources for records (birth, death, marriage and divorce), but is more complete. *Records* gives addresses for more problematic concerns like where to write for records on U.S. citizens born outside this country and the addresses of various foreign embassies. The lagniappe is the inclusion of some actual clip-out forms.

3. Nemeth, Charles. *Private Security and the Investigative Process*, Cincinnati: Anderson, 1992. Nemeth supplies a great deal of technical data. This book is especially helpful in providing copies of forms on everything from the "Investigator's Daily Report of Investigation" to "Consent to Search." Nemeth also details how to collect, pack and mark physical evidence.

Of course, some people are missing without knowing they are missing. Distant heirs, occasional witnesses and biological parents fall into this category. Because they have such a distant or tenuous relationship to the persons wanting them found, they are often the most difficult to locate, but they do fall in the province of the PI.

Here are some major categories of missing persons:

Skip Traces. Movies and TV often focus on the person who takes off after making bail — hence, the term "skips" — so the bail bondsman hires the Bounty Hunter or the Fall Guy to "bring 'em back alive." But skips are also people like the subcontractor who starts the atrium, takes the initial payment, and vanishes. Most are not career criminals who make a living moving from town to town bilking unsuspecting victims. Most skips simply change their address but not their profession and hence can be located through their work.

Runaways. Most true runaways are teens who can no longer cope at home. In recent years wives have left home because of some form of spousal abuse. Older men and women, victims of stress, suddenly pull up stakes and flee. People who have moved beyond mere stress and into real mental problems also run. Most such persons, though, are not pros and do not really know what they are doing or how to do it well.

Attorney-Related. Lawyers often hire PIs to locate people for various legal reasons. Sometimes lawyers need to find the person who befriended their Howard Hughes-type client, and, for some reason, they don't trust phone-ins to TV shows like *America's Greatest Unclaimed Fortunes*. More often, it's a minor bequest, for usually in the case of large sums, heirs appear like vultures before their "favorite" uncle expires.

Witnesses come in two types—those who have attested to something of their own free will and those who have stumbled upon accidents/crimes. Obviously the more voluntary the witness, the easier s/he is to locate. People who notice a crime in progress are often reluctant to come forward. Much of the time such witnesses aren't even known to exist until an investigator has gotten thoroughly involved in a case.

John recently had a case where a witness to a fatal accident had gone to the police at the scene and given them what he thought was his business card. Actually it was of someone he had met at a convention. Moreover, that person had never even been in the state where the accident occurred. The police accident report listed Mr. X as a witness, but when questioned, X was dumbfounded as to how his name and card had turned up.

John investigated. Through persistent questioning, he learned that Mr. X had attended a convention of roadway engineers in Atlanta the week before the fatal accident. A canvas showed two registered highway engineers in the town where the accident occurred. One of them, shaken by having seen the accident, had inadvertently handed the overworked traffic cop the card Mr. X had given him in Atlanta. With the witness in place, the client's lawyer won the case and presented John with a $2,500 bonus check (though the case was settled for a million).

Security

In the old days the Pinkertons protected the railroads. Nowadays, detectives rarely do security work, because, in this age of specialization, colleges give degrees in Loss Prevention, Fire Security, etc. As a result, large businesses have their own security divisions and draw their recruits from college graduates.

At the other end of the scale is the Rent-A-Badge. These are essentially hired guns who patrol an area to keep it secure. Most large cities have firms that supply rent-a-cops. Because some states have little or no laws governing this industry, those involved often have little or no law enforcement training. Many carry weapons they haven't been adequately trained to use; few have investigative skills. In the strictest sense, such people are protectors, not detectives.

But PIs still do some security work. One main area is that of bodyguard (or "hard men" as they like to call themselves). Even in this area, schools that train guards in protecting celebrities, businessmen and their families have sprung up; often such schools emphasize a single skill like driving or firearms. Robert Parker has used Spenser to guard a lesbian author and a Christian Senator, which is possible since pros rarely let their own politics (assuming they have any) interfere in their job. In real life, John has guarded such celebrities as Telly Savalas, Farrah Fawcett, Lee Majors and Jeff Bridges.

From time to time John has been hired as a bodyguard. In one case a woman used him not just to protect her from an ex-husband, but actually set up the situation so that John would hopefully kill the ex. Fortunately, John caught on to her scam, resisting her liquor, her charm, and a long prison sentence. In one of his strangest cases, John contracted to guard a hole in the ground in the eastern Kentucky mountains where a gas pipeline had exploded. Large gas companies are a natural target for people who might fall in excavation or accident sites, drive their car in, or are "looking for a check." This scam is usually run by people looking for early retirement. Unfortunately for John, although the gas company had told him they had experienced some recent "unpleasantness," they had neglected to mention that their employees were on strike. One morning while sitting beside the hole John discovered how "unpleasant" the workers were when a bullet knocked his Thermos off a makeshift table. Luckily, the guy was shooting at the Thermos or John wouldn't be around to talk about it.

A growing aspect of security is electronic espionage and counterespionage. Since the former is a federal offense (and often a state as well), most PIs would claim they're engaging in the latter to prevent the former. Here industrial specialists and high tech equipment are called for, but a PI might be used to bug a place or sweep a place for bugs (see chapter nine for details on this kind of equipment). However, the average small-town PI, while being able to obtain this equipment, is probably not going to be an expert with it nor able to justify a huge expenditure for rarely used technology. DAK Industries makes a device for less than a hundred dollars that can detect taps on a phone, but bugs today can be the size of a strand of hair; some are powered by the subject's household wiring and are undetectable by conventional means. In all probability, should sophisticated electronic equipment be needed, a specialist will be called in (see chapter sixteen on hired help).

Patricia Holt's *The Bug in the Martini Olive* is an in-depth look at an electronics surveillance expert, PI Hal Lipset of San Francisco. Along the way Holt explains eavesdropping law, the variety of equipment, and many of Lipset's cases.

A PI often enters the security field through background checks. Sometimes a potential employee is a question mark; other times a current employee might be designated a risk with additional information needed. It's the job of the PI, through personal observation and research, to ferret out the truth. Chapter thirteen explains how such a check is carried out.

PIs will be hired from outside a company because they are objective or in the right place at the time. A business in California once hired John to run a background check on an applicant who had attended the University of Kentucky. Another possibility is using a PI to test a group's security or examine an executive's itinerary for vulnerable areas — possible assassination sites, hotels in the wrong section of town, known enemies in the area.

Insurance

The National Insurance Crime Bureau estimates that false and inflated claims cost $17 billion a year. Large insurance companies generally have their own investigators. Also, sometimes a Pennsylvania-based company of any size may need some work done in Alabama. Oftentimes with large sums of money in question and some unanswered questions about the circumstances of the accident, companies hire a local PI to research a claimant's charges. This area is becoming so specialized that some agencies do nothing but investigate claims for worker's compensation.

Arson

Insurance companies often use PIs for arson investigation. Large city police will have a trained squad, but small towns may not even have one nearby. Sometimes even large insurance companies become dissatisfied with official arson reports. The PI enters the case not to search for potential incendiary devices — that's the province of on-the-scene professionals who look for and examine physical evidence using sophisticated electronic "sniffers" — but to investigate the victims of fires, especially their finances. Also, since some arson is motivated by revenge, the detective might be asked to come up with a list of those who bore a grudge against the insured victim and to investigate them. Finally, a detective might be asked to canvas the neighborhood of the fire to determine if anybody noticed any suspicious behavior.

John once investigated a woman suspected of burning down her home. He solved the case by finding a cache of her kids' memorabilia she had hidden so the fire wouldn't get them. Experience has taught John that parents hate to part with pictures of their children.

Collecting

Two major areas of this field are bad checks and repos. In the movies, bill collectors and repo men are often behemoth hulks named Vinnie or Vito with an I.Q. equivalent to their shoe size. And although collection agencies dominate this scene through writing harassing computerized letters and making repeated boilerroom calls (cold calls made by temporary hires), PIs are often used, especially in smaller towns. While a collection agency investigator most often works on a percentage basis, a detective usually receives a flat fee for every car or bill s/he collects from a welcher. Most PIs dislike this kind of work because with credit so easy to obtain (even cable TV advertises a "guaranteed" credit card for ten dollars), they're never sure of what kind of person or situation they'll run into. John has found that since the Carter administration required institutions to be less restrictive about mental patients, he seems to have inadvertently located a great many of them.

An emerging area of collections is the deadbeat parent, the man or woman who refuses to pay court-ordered child support. The U.S. Census estimates that by the end of 1989 such parents were in arrears for $19 billion. Fay Faron, a forty-two-year-old PI and owner of the Rat Dog Dick Detective Agency in San Francisco, likes this kind of work. In fact, in her *A Private Eye's Guide to Collecting a Bad*

Debt (San Francisco: Creighton-Morgan, 1991), she includes tips on how the average person can collect such monies.

Divorce

Police generally consider domestic disputes one of the most dangerous situations to step into. PIs look at divorce work the same way because unlike most other specialties, the emotions are naturally intense and raw. On the other hand, with the divorce rate in this country hovering around 50 percent, there's a lot of work out there for the detective.

Working in a small town, John finds the divorce problem acute. He knows many of the people involved in a marital breakup, their backgrounds, their family histories and their lifelong relationships that are often more complex than genetically engineered compounds. He gets cussed out in public by strangers, some who merely assume he was the PI in the spouse's case. More often than he likes to think about, he finds himself working for, say, a man's wife when a few years earlier he took a case involving the husband. Interestingly, his very first case was for a woman whose husband had disappeared. One day, seven years after she had had him declared legally dead, she looked out the window of a Louisville bus, and there he was just walking down the street carrying a racing form. She quickly hired John to find him, both for emotional and legal reasons.

One basic lesson is that all divorce work is not "true" divorce work—often an investigation precedes or follows the breakup. John has learned a more painful lesson. No matter how well he knows the clients, no matter what the distraught wife offers him, or no matter how much he empathizes with a party, he must remember: *don't get emotionally involved.* Objectivity and success are usually directly proportional to distance.

Once again, each state manages to develop its own set of divorce laws. So, find out if your detective operates in a common-law state. Are dissolutions legal? Joint custody? Check out the "grounds," but realize they are not the only concern. Many times a man or woman on first meeting with John begins the interview with "I'm suspicious of my mate." Usually some new form of behavior (often involving the bedroom) has them curious. What they claim they want to know is what's really going on. In truth, they know the answer, but want the detective to do something about it. At various times they ask John to be Dr. Joyce Brothers, Allan Funt, Johnny Wadd and a Mafioso mechanic.

Lawyers also contact PIs for divorce work. Sometimes they need help in proving "grounds"; sometimes they need to be sure their client's spouse has played fair and provided a reasonably accurate list of assets; sometimes they need to establish the degree of depravity of the other spouse so the client can get child custody, alimony, child support or Aunt Minnie's pearl comb set.

A problem your PI should be aware of is corroboration, people who can support his/her claims. Courts tend to believe the side that has been able to line up the most witnesses, people who verify the side's contentions. The PI often needs a partner other than the trusty camcorder, a person who can substantiate that Subject A was in Cafe B at 1:00 A.M. And so expenses, like emotions, run high.

Why with all the pain, danger and expense involved do PIs continue to do divorce work? Because the seventh commandment is violated so often, adultery has become our nation's number one crime, and crime pays. One PI estimates the average divorce case is worth $4,000.

John thinks most PIs realize how volatile divorce situations are, and a responsible, professional PI is very careful about how and when to present potentially inflammatory evidence to a client. Every now and then, though, a Dorothy Stratton case develops. Dorothy's husband, worried that his wife, former *Playboy* Playmate of the Year, was cheating on him, hired a detective. Upon seeing the evidence the detective gathered, the husband killed her.

Some detectives won't touch domestic work. Ed Hino, for instance, thinks there's too much sleaze involved in it and for the most part turns down clients desiring such investigations.

1-900-INFIDEL

Philandering spouses take note. PI Bill Colligan of Encino, California, has created the Infidelity Hotline. For $2 a minute, you can call to take the Suspicion Evaluation Quiz. Usually Colligan, who for thirty-one years was a detective specializing in divorce, advises against hiring an investigator, preferring simply to counsel you himself. Warning: Colligan has been married three times.

What type of person most cheats on their mate? Doctors.

Child Custody

While child custody used to be an outgrowth of divorce work, John has found that it's also become a large field in itself. Sometimes, for instance, it's the grandparents who want custody. And each state's related laws can affect the PI. In Kentucky, for example, a parent cannot go back to court for custody unless new evidence is discovered. Most often this evidence consists of the harm contention — that is, the PI is hired to locate evidence that the custodial parent may do the child harm or expose him/her to a dangerous situation. Another problem in this state is that if noncustodial parents snatch their own kid, the most they can be charged with is a misdemeanor; thus, they can't be extradited from other states (only felonies lead to extradition). Even the federal Uniform Child Custody Act isn't a guarantee of help in another state. John remembers a case in which he located the noncustodial snatcher in Indiana, showed the sheriff the custody order, but the female sheriff refused to help him take a child away from its natural mother.

Bounty Hunting

While bounty hunters can trace skips, their hunting range is larger. They will pursue felons — bank robbers, murderers, con men. When John was starting out, he put meat on the table by working for five years for bail bondsmen and tracking down bail jumpers. More recently, he has located embezzlers of fidelity bonds. He once caught a real estate agent who was stealing escrow funds. However, legislation in Kentucky did away with the trade and put John out of work. Again, make sure if you have your PI in this line of work, it is legal in the detective's state.

Odd Jobs

While no PI we know has yet been hired to discover who put the "bomp" in the "bomp-she-bomp" or whether Lite beer is truly less filling or simply tastes great, detectives are occasionally retained for offbeat services.

One such job is process serving, which is normally handled by law enforcement officials. Once again, you the writer have to know the state law covering your fictional case. Can your detective legally act as a process server? If so, what special acts and fee would allow him/her to perform this job? Also, if the answer is yes, is it legal for your detective to tail a person to serve the subpoena? New York law, for instance, specifically has ruled that the shadowing of "a person by a private detective for the purpose of serving a subpoena has been held not to constitute a crime." A Wisconsin process serving firm recently hired John to serve a subpoena on a Tulsa truck driver who was wanted for hit and run and was supposedly living in Kentucky.

John has also been asked to locate two horses. In another instance he was asked to find the UFO that was tattooing an elderly farmer's cattle. Once a couple claimed they were being watched, their mail censored, and objects in their home were being turned to odd angles. How long? asked John. For more than twenty-five years, the couple said. It's the only case of dual delusion John has ever experienced.

Detectives can act as go-betweens. A PI might be hired to go to another state, pick up a package of valuable military miniatures and bring it back. Security and speed make the PI into a glorified delivery boy, and money often makes the detective more tight-lipped and involved than a bonded courier. Blackmail is another possibility as is helping in the exchange of a kidnap victim. In fact, the reputation of the individual detective concerning this specialty is often the reason s/he's asked. John has been asked a few times, and one of the rare kidnap cases he has ever said no to involved making the exchange in Argentina. Another time local thieves stole some valuables. When they read in the newspaper that one of the purloined items was a Picasso-autographed napkin, something difficult to fence in Kentucky, they contacted John about an exchange. The thieves picked the back lot of a local supermarket as the spot. While they were sitting on the roof, covering John with shotguns as he was looking under boxes for the loot, a bag boy emerged and accused John of stealing pop cases.

Suppose you've thought about your PI getting involved with labor unions. One more time: *check your state's law*. A fictional Empire State investigator who looks into a walkout by the Amalgamated Widget Workers of America (AWWA) is operating illegally. New York law, for instance, prohibits PIs from "interfering or participating in strikes or other matters involving organized labor."

The specialty for the 1990s is mate-checking. While this sounds like something the zoo would do for Hugo the gorilla, people in this AIDS-conscious age hire PIs to look into their future mate's health background, marital and financial status, and education. Jerry Palace and Tim Bartlett, retired New York City police detectives, operate such a service, Check-a-Mate.

Another burgeoning field is political investigations. In 1991 Bill Clinton hired Ace Smith, a San Francisco PI, to perform "opposition research" (translation: how much dirt can be dug up). Smith's target was Clinton himself as the Arkansas governor wanted to know in advance what his vulnerable areas were. Little Rock, Arkansas, private detective Larry Case, on the other hand, claimed he was on the payrolls of several national news organizations to check out Clinton's past life.

Another growth area is background checking job applicants, which involves interviewing friends, neighbors and previous employers. Because he worked previously for the FBI, Ed Hino specializes in this kind of job. Glamorous, it is not. In fact, Ed says he spends a great deal of time simply filing forms with the Pennsylvania Department of Transportation to check on an applicant's driving record or with the State Police to locate criminal records. Interestingly, he has been told a few times *not* to ask if the applicant has a prior history of drugs or mental problems.

How specific can an agency's focus be? Diligence Inc. claims it can trace the life of an NBA draft prospect back to grade school.

Summary

Small-town PIs, like small-town doctors and lawyers, are often jacks-of-all-trades. Versatility by necessity. Even new detectives in large city firms, if not corporate operations, serve whatever client comes through the door. As a writer, then, you must have a clear idea of your detective's given character, his/her location (small town, big city), and his/her state to create cases that ring true.

Hints

1. To see what areas of specialization exist, the names of actual firms, the products available to such specialists, the journals they read, the organizations to which they belong, and specific

"consultants" in everything from antiterrorism to drug testing, see the *Security Letter SourceBook* (New York: Security Letter, annual), but you may have trouble finding it at a local library. College libraries, especially if the school has some sort of law enforcement major, will probably carry it.

2. If your PI is involved in an area requiring specific technical expertise (e.g., electronic surveillance), you probably won't be able to gather sufficient in-depth information from a mere reading in the field. You will have to consult an expert who has the depth of background knowledge, is up-to-date on state-of-the-art equipment, and has practical experience handling the equipment as well as interacting with authorities. In other words, the more specific the area, the greater the need to personally contact a PI.

F I V E

THE OFFICE

*Opening the door to my office, I said hello to Mary Lou, good-bye heart.
My secretary was hunched over her word processor but focused on the
National Inquirer. I entered my inner sanctum. Overhead, my ceiling
fan was losing another battle to the heavy, stale air. The walls were barer
than a stripper's butt and twice as dirty. That wasn't my fault. Cleaning
services wouldn't come into this section of town.*

*Ritualistically I opened my filing drawer. What I needed most was
there under C for cognac. It was also there under H for Hennessey's
and M for Martell.*

Richard Steele,
Josh Shepherd, PI

The first thing you should know about an office is that many PIs,
especially small-towners, don't have one — at least not in the traditional sense. In fact, many PIs operate out of their homes. Now,
admittedly, having fictional scenes where the blonde in trouble
slowly drives into the cozy subdivision may not seem exciting, but at
least the locale is accurate. William Pearce, a Virginia detective
who specializes in divorce cases, admits that although he has several
rented offices, he does most of his work at home. The rentals are
mainly for show.

Why no downtown office? Part of the problem is that with an
office where the public can easily walk in, the PI gets little work
done. More important, many clients don't want to be seen entering
the office of a private investigator. It may start questions; it may just
prove embarrassing ("Why, dear, we didn't realize *you* were having
problems."). In this respect, PIs get less respect than Rodney Dan-
gerfield and psychiatrists combined.

As mentioned earlier, John's current office is in the second floor of a downtown bank. Clients can easily walk into the bank as if they are about to perform some routine financial transaction and take the elevator up. Sometimes clients do come by his home, but they're usually good clients he's invited there. Roughly half of his initial meetings with clients, as well as subsequent interviews, take place at local restaurants. John has a real preference for Frisch's Big Boy because it's always open, he can see what's going on, and they refill his coffee without his asking.

Physical Plant

Ideally a detective's office, if not a private residence, is located in an easily accessible area. This usually means Main Street or just off it. When Hal and Charlie were writing the Mike Shayne stories, they were forced by their editor to stick to the series' "bible." This guidebook for ghosts declared that the "rawboned redhead" maintained an office on Flagler Street near the Orange Bowl. In the late 1930s when the series started, that might have been a solid address in a prosperous neighborhood. But by the late 1980s even the NFL Dolphins had fled to the suburbs. In truth, Mike wasn't going to get a lot of walk-in trade, his clients weren't going to park their expensive cars out front, and his beautiful secretary, Lucy, wasn't going to feel safe leaving the office after working late.

If your sense of business is on a par with your knowledge of laparoscopy, you might still decide to create a detective who, like you, knows little about business. In truth, such detectives may be the rule. "Most private eyes just don't know how to run a business," says Roger E. Boswarva, a New York private investigator. Todd Taylor, co-author of a recent study on the growth of private security firms, claims that most small PI firms fold because they are run by former law enforcement personnel who lack business experience or marketing skills. Moreover, they are underfinanced and have a small client base usually left over from their law enforcement days. A caveat: The trick is for you, the writer, to maintain control; don't unwittingly allow, for instance, your businessperson-PI to make some amateurish financial blunder.

Office Equipment

While field work often necessitates specialized and expensive equipment (see chapter nine), the PI can get by with the basics. A telephone is essential. In the home office, the PI uses a separate line for tax purposes. Even though the latest Sears *Wish Book* lists a fax for $399, the machine is a luxury. If faxing is needed, most towns have businesses that charge for individual calls. And while the trusty typewriter looks good on the desk (another essential), the small computer with printer looks better. It's certainly more efficient, necessitates less storage space (though it would be harder for Josh Shepherd to hide his cognac among the floppy disks), and provides better copies. Moreover, if you suffer with John's spelling problem (he is, in his own words, "profoudly dexlaic"), Spelchek is more effective than Webster's. Basic desk supplies, phone books and a filing cabinet also help.

And don't be like Shepherd and forget that one frame on the wall. No, it won't contain a picture of your PI's Susan Silverman or Velda, but the detective's license.

Secretary

While it's nice to have somebody to type up reports, file them and answer the phone, your PI does not need a Lucy Hamilton. The PI can use a cheap answering machine or even an answering service. Yes, doctors and drug dealers aren't the only ones with beepers. Besides, without a secretary, your PI doesn't have to pay worker's comp or social security.

Insurance

And speaking of insurance, as we noted earlier with obtaining a license, various states require different types and amounts of insurance; common sense requires others. One more time: *check your particular state*. Any local insurance agent can fill you in. In general, three types of insurance are usually necessary.

Surety bond. Obtained through a bonding company. Basically the bond protects the PI's clients. Should the detective fail to live up to contractual agreements, the bonding company pays. Of course, the detective is required to make an initial investment.

Liability insurance. Purchased from an insurance company, protects the PI. Should a detective injure any person or property during a case, the insurance company compensates the injured party.

Haven't you ever wondered who pays for the damage caused by Thomas Magnum, Mike Hammer or Spenser during all those obligatory car chase scenes? The truth is that the TV detectives, had they insurance, would have their policies cancelled or rates skyrocket after the damage their chases cause. If they didn't have insurance, they'd be out of business or running it from the local lockup.

Worker's comp. Provides payment for a PI injured in the course of the job. While most real-life detectives aren't injured in car chases, accidents in other areas do occur.

In fact, when John thinks about his chances of being killed or injured in just normal work, what do you think he considers the greatest single risk to which he is exposed? Driving. "You find yourself driving around distracted. Your mind is on what you are doing, not on your driving, and you find yourself in a strange neighborhood looking for an address." A detective has a small comfort zone. The car for the PI becomes a surrogate office. Sometimes the only way John sees his clients is in a parking lot or garage after setting it up on the phone. Sometimes clients pick up John in their car. His latest gadget, thrust on him by his bank employers and now his trusty companion, is not a partner but a cellular phone.

Also, John notes that occasionally he is involved in fender benders. He has had a few cars shot up, and, yes, Holy Cecil B. deMille, he has been involved in a few car chases. But when he gets involved in "heavy" cases that he feels might lead to such conclusions, he usually rents a vehicle from Hertz or Budget and carries a full load of insurance.

Other Business Expenses

Sooner or later every PI needs legal advice, if not representation. PIs get sued by clients as well as by people they have been investigating. They have to go before boards, and they testify in court. Maybe they need an attorney just to discover if their neighborhood is zoned for home offices. Moreover, a PI is often no more adept than any other citizen at interpreting civil codes and particular statutes. PIs need lawyers to get them started in business for such things as checking rental agreements. And the law is constantly changing through legislatures, local referendums, city commissions and higher court decisions — staying *au courant* is oh so difficult.

John points out that if your detective is older or experienced, he will often seek out a good lawyer with lots of "street smarts." Such attorneys have been around long enough to have established a network. They know which judges, which policemen, which doctors to seek out. The axiom "who you know" still holds.

Just as most Americans turn to H&R Block, detectives also need accounting help. Agencies have payrolls to meet and taxes to pay on a regular basis. Legitimate deductions and business expenses are a problem. How much mileage will the IRS allow to be written off? If the office is at home, what percent of the mortgage, light bill and heating is deductible? Should the PI incorporate? Tax planning, retirement and 401-K's are something each of us considers, and detectives are no different.

Summary

No, you don't need to clutter up a good piece of PI fiction with the detective unable to concentrate on finding the Jenkins baby because worker's comp is due on the fifteenth. As the writer, however, you should be aware of these concerns. Such knowledge not only aids believability, but opens avenues of plot development. What if your PI is being hounded worse than the Church of Scientology claims they are by the IRS? Suppose while your detective is working to get evidence that a local factory is guilty of dumping toxic waste, the neighborhood association is trying to get the city to remove an unauthorized business — the detective's — from their subdivision?

Hints

1. If your PI has an office, personalize it. We've noted only the bare necessities of an office, but what about the decor? We're not suggesting you become an interior decorator, but you need to have accessories in the office that reflect the PI's personality. Perhaps there are photos of the PI's previous life — FBI class, Army buddies, receiving a medal of valor from the police force. A hard-boiled PI probably won't put posters on the walls. Is the office neat? Are there trophies? Do the file cabinets match the desk? If a PI has a neat rolltop desk, will that tell the reader more than the standard metal desk? A detective who trumpets

success with newspaper clippings and awards is different from one who has only four bare walls.

2. Know your detective's financial situation. If you claim your PI has an office on the corner of Fourth and Maple in downtown Akron, find out what such a place goes for in the time period of your setting. What would the insurance be? What kind of neighborhood is Fourth and Maple? Does the building have any security? Is it a firetrap that would be uninviting for walk-in traffic?

3. Part-time help costs money. Down-and-out habitual drunks who rarely get paid for their cases can't afford accountants and part-time surveillance help.

ADVERTISING

I spent the rest of the morning sitting under Kleig lights that were hotter than a streetwalker's first kiss. The Bishop Agency was shooting a thirty-second spot for local cable to, as they put it, "increase my client base." The commercial was an integral part of my comprehensive marketing strategy, following on the heels of my full-page ad in the Yellow Pages (in shocking red, of course, and featuring a large bloodshot eye, a Thompson submachine gun, and me in my trenchcoat holding a magnifying glass). We'd also hired some local kids to put my fancy flyers under the windshield wipers of every car parked downtown. Then there were my business cards, the well-placed graffiti in local restrooms . . .

Richard Steele,
Josh Shepherd, PI

Obviously private investigation is a business, and like most businesses it needs advertising to succeed. The key to effective advertising is location. As a general rule, small-town PIs rely less on traditional, and even nontraditional, advertising formats than their metropolitan counterparts. Large-city firms often do take out ads in the Yellow Pages. The most important information given out here is the areas in which the firm specializes. Some agencies advertise general services such as the types of cases they handle — e.g., domestic, civil. Other firms provide more specific details like Air Crash Investigations, Handwriting Comparisons, and Patents and Trademarks. In cities large enough to have different area codes, potential clients have many choices, so offering a large variety of specified services provides an opportunity to attract many clients.

Word of Mouth vs. Formal Methods

Medium-sized firms and one-person ops like the Josh Shepherd Agency rarely resort to a "comprehensive marketing strategy" that includes flyers, videotapes, not to mention graffiti in the johns. Small-town agencies, especially where there's only one in town, might not use the Yellow Pages at all. For instance, the only place John is listed in the Richmond phone book is under his home address — and without any hint of his profession. "The trouble with advertising," he says, "is you open yourself up to every kook who stops at the Holiday Inn and gets your number." So how does he get his name around? Word of mouth, which he finds is the most effective advertising possible in a small town. Not only does his name get passed around, but the longer he works, the more often he gets recommendations from satisfied clients.

John has also uncovered an inexplicable phenomenon. Even in cases he has screwed up or just been unable to complete, he finds the clients still give him a good recommendation. As a result, when potential clients are contemplating hiring him, he usually gives them a list of people he has helped (and who have previously agreed to talk about it) and encourages them to call. Unfortunately, to preserve confidentiality some of his best work remains anonymous.

But even word of mouth has its down side. With all the cases he has worked and the contacts made, John has quite a local reputation. More than once he has been working a stakeout when someone has recognized him and asked something like, "Hey, what's Richmond's most famous PI working on now?" From that point on, his cover blown, John's truthful response is, "Nothing."

John is most often recommended by the local police. He has worked a great many cases with them, knows most of the officers personally, and has even employed some of them when they were off-duty. And though it may seem like a cliché, a lot of officers share John's interest in exotic women and weapons. But even such a working relationship is a double-edged sword. Sure, when a person comes to the police with something outside their jurisdiction — usually a domestic problem — the cop shop points them to the next block and John's office. But occasionally when "a nut case" shows up at the station house complaining "The neighbor's poodle won't stop talking to me," they'll let slip that John has successfully handled other talking dog cases.

John will never forget one case. A man called the State Police to warn that his girlfriend, then heading down the interstate, was determined to jump from a high bridge. When a trooper spotted her and pulled up behind her, she sprayed herself with lighter fluid and set herself on fire. The trooper pulled her over and saved her life. When the man asked the trooper whom he would recommend to help such persons, the obliging cop didn't choose a psychologist. That night the man showed up on John's doorstep claiming, "I'm in danger. If my girlfriend can't kill herself, I'm next." This is exactly the kind of visitor every PI loves.

The truth is that the essential nature of investigation is often secretive. Most clients desire confidentiality. They don't want other people to know John is working for them, and often a high-profile detective won't be sought out by clients because his very image seems to scream "Publicity!" How would you feel if that very private investigation you had done last year suddenly showed up as the headline story on *American Detectives*?

Rotten Apple—The Mine-Salter

Rather than rely on advertising or word of mouth to keep his caseload full, this rotten apple uses a more direct approach. He creates a case himself, then brings it to the client. The potential heir is a favorite game ("You may be a distant relative to the fortune of the recently deceased Howard X"). Salters have been known to use former clients they have determined to be gullible.

Once the salter has hooked the client, various methods are used to work the "mark." Just when the case (and the client's money) seems to be drying up, the salter will conveniently uncover just the piece of evidence needed to revive the client's interest. Or, with a particularly naive client, the salter might even claim to discover information that points in an entirely new direction and, of course, requires just a little more money to "follow up."

Business Cards

All detectives carry business cards. It is important to be able to leave with people a compact form of information for later reference. Most large firms use the traditional white card with block black letters and no logos—i.e., very businesslike. Often the name of the firm does not scream *detective*. "Security" is a favorite euphemism. United Intelligence, Inc. sounds like a think tank. Intertech, Inc.

could be a computer specialist, and The Ackerman Group sounds like an insurance conglomerate. These cards usually provide the firm's name, address, phone number, perhaps a specialty and the agent's name.

As a small-town PI, John is in the position of having to wear many hats, and only one is a deerstalker. So, because many different types of requests come across his desk, he has several business cards, each geared for a particular clientele. Like a quarterback looking

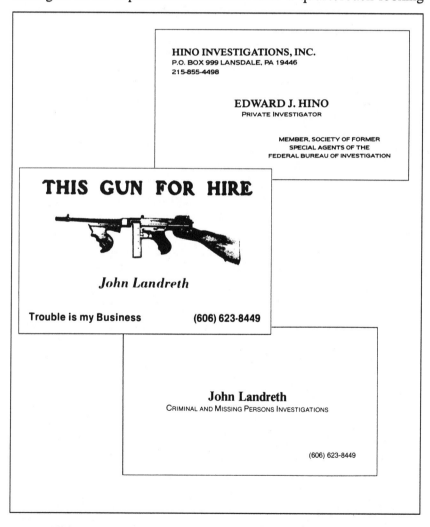

HINO INVESTIGATIONS, INC.
P.O. BOX 999 LANSDALE, PA 19446
215-855-4498

EDWARD J. HINO
PRIVATE INVESTIGATOR

MEMBER, SOCIETY OF FORMER
SPECIAL AGENTS OF THE
FEDERAL BUREAU OF INVESTIGATION

THIS GUN FOR HIRE

John Landreth

Trouble is my Business   (606) 623-8449

John Landreth
CRIMINAL AND MISSING PERSONS INVESTIGATIONS

(606) 623-8449

Calling cards used by private investigators come in a variety of styles.

over a defense, he "reads" a client, then produces the appropriate card. For corporate clients, for instance, he hands out a calm white card with just his name, business address and business number.

But he has other cards and their origins are interesting. A couple of years ago John successfully completed a violent crime investigation for a coal tipple operator in eastern Kentucky. Noticing that John had only the simple business card, the client decided that his favorite detective needed a more graphic card to deal with the "good old boy crowd" who equate the size of a man's character with the proportions of the weapon he carries. And obviously, decided the client, John had loads of character. A month later John opened a package to find a white card with all the requisite business information printed under the logo of a Thompson submachine gun like the ones carried by Hoover's G-Men. Below the logo, a slogan declared *Trouble Is My Business. This Gun For Hire.* At first John was a little wary of the impression such a melodramatic card would leave with a prospective client. Reluctantly he tried it out on a few clients, and to his amazement it worked—beautifully. Now, the first (traditional) card is for clients wanting a PI who's smart and efficient—a thinker. The second is for someone who's enamored by the image of the hard-boiled PI whose ultimate solution to solving a case involves fists or a gat.

Recently a very satisfied female client gave John a third card. The face is a night scene. A PI in a trenchcoat adds drama to the background. In the foreground is the backside of a seminude female (the client) baring, among other things, a submachine gun. Across the bottom appear the words "Expose the Bare Facts and Get to the Bottom of Things." John claims this is purely a novelty card.

Sure. And all PIs wear Hawaiian shirts just like Magnum.

Other Methods

Some detectives have found other ways to generate favorable publicity. William Callahan has enjoyed positive exposure in the *Wall Street Journal* and *USA Today*, the two largest national papers. Jay J. Armes had a TV pilot made about his adventures. Marilyn Greene, Irwin Blye and Josiah Thompson have written books, as well as appeared on TV talk shows and radio. Some detectives establish a rapport with reporters for local papers to get positive stories (when confidentiality is not threatened). Some PIs give out personalized novelty items such as ashtrays, magnifying glasses, meerschaum pipes and pornographic business cards.

Summary

A detective must get the word out that s/he is a mousetrap, if not the better mousetrap. A major problem with the credibility of much detective fiction today is that almost never do the detectives advertise. Would people really come to a run-down office on the bad side of town because they just happened to hear that Josh Shepherd was open for business? Maybe, if Josh, like a lot of other fictional detectives, was never seen being paid for his work.

Hints

1. Check out the Yellow Pages of a major city phone book (found in local/university libraries) for ads placed by PIs. Note the varying sizes, the graphic design and the specialties noted. Is an address listed? PIs with phone numbers only—no address—have a greater chance of being fly-by-night operations and are definitely smaller ops.

2. If your PI has a Yellow Pages ad, match it up to his/her personality. Flamboyant PIs would have a more colorful, eye-catching ad—large letters, logo, slogan. This matching also applies to business cards.

APPEARANCE

The shoot over, I stepped into the john to check out my look. The cracked mirror shot back the image of a man in control. An untorched Camel dangled from my lips. Black turtleneck, expensive madras sportcoat, creased chinos, patent leathers, Bogie trenchcoat. I was everything the well-dressed private detective ought to be.

Richard Steele,
Josh Shepherd, PI

Does a detective's appearance really matter? Doesn't a client hire a PI for results and reputation rather than looks? Can't a lead be pursued in a pair of L.A. Gears or Bally loafers? Does the situation dictate the detective's precise dress? Yes.

The Suit

When Allan Pinkerton got started, he required his operatives to dress in coats and ties, since upper-echelon cops wore that at the time. While today there is no one standard detective outfit and no universal dress code that mandates fedora and trenchcoat, appropriate dress still applies. As previously emphasized, the private eye has become more and more a businessperson, a "suit." Wearing a dark business suit (or its female equivalent) certainly makes sense when the PI deals with the corporate business world, but what about the other times?

About 95 percent of the time, John wears a white shirt, club tie and dark suit. He thinks it important, even when dealing with Low-Life Scum, to look in control. Sure, there are times when he's running around and changes to more casual, comfortable and appropriate attire, but most of the time, if he doesn't know his client or what the day holds, he dons the suit.

On more than one occasion John has had a client or an adversary tell him, "You don't look like a detective." Which brings up some interesting questions. What does a detective look like? Does a detective really want to look like what a PI is seen as looking like?

The answer depends on the situation. When John first meets a client, obviously he wants to look like a PI. But not the TV/movie variety. Since most people want to hire someone who appears smart, professional and prosperous, he tries to look the part. On the other hand, when he has someone under surveillance, he wants to be able to blend in. When he interviews people, whether those in power (lawyers, real estate agents, judges) or those not, he gets more respect and information out of a suit than jeans, a T-shirt and Nikes.

Does a PI have a look? No more than a banker or other businessperson. PIs probably won't be mistaken for stevedores or interior designers, but they are not easily identifiable as gumshoes either.

Is there a difference between what a PI wears in the office and in the field? Since a detective usually works several cases at once, it would be impractical if not impossible to switch wardrobes for each job. John finds the suit is going to be appropriate more often than not. Besides, with a coat and tie, if he descends a few steps on the social and evolutionary ladder, it's easy to remove the coat, loosen the tie, roll up the sleeves, and at least look as casual as somebody running for office.

Ed Hino dresses according to the situation. If he meets a client in a restaurant, he wears a shirt and tie. When searching courthouse records, he dons what he would on a golf course (sans spiked shoes). For most interviews he puts on a sports coat and tie. But if he's going to see a lawyer client, he wears a suit and tie.

Accessories

Specific articles of clothing do matter. Unless your detective works full-time for Donald Trump or IBM, a good outfit would be a wash-and-wear suit—something cheap, easy to clean and maintain. Josh

Shepherd's patent leathers clash with the rest of his outfit, they can become really uncomfortable if he has a day of pounding the pavement, and they don't hold up. A good pair of comfortable shoes is extremely important. Only in TV and movies where PIs run 100-meter dashes after the bad guys are sneakers always appropriate. Real-life private investigator Irwin Blye points out that his biggest single expense is shoes. John is a great believer in Florsheim boots. Not only do they provide comfort, but also protect his ankles. Since John has been in five car crashes and one helicopter crash, this detail is quite important. When he got in the business, many police detectives wore Florsheim Imperials. Young detectives today, he finds, often wear chukka boots with white socks, betraying their patrolman origins.

And Shepherd's trenchcoat and madras jacket would only do a good job of helping him stand out in the crowd, which usually isn't desirable. The turtleneck might be suitable unless Shepherd operates in a Southern city, but at least he's not wearing a highly starched shirt, which can get very uncomfortable on days and nights of long surveillance. A strong belt is important since so many PIs wear clip-on holsters. In fact, John's found that worn spots on the belt above the hip are a dead giveaway of a cop/PI.

John, though, is a staunch defender of the trenchcoat, especially the classic London Fog. Tan is a better color than the black coats that dominated the 1960s because tan is appropriate for so many places. The coat is perfect in inclement weather, it's perfect for wearing in cars, it helps when he's not sure whether there's a chance of showers (snow or otherwise), and he can wear it into interviewees' homes. In those times when he definitely wants to be perceived as a PI, the coat helps the image. In dangerous situations John can put his hands in his pockets and get at weapons through the pocket slits. The coat is bulky enough so that he can hide weapons without them being seen.

Glasses are another concern. Now that he's older and his eyes are going, going, gone, John wears contacts. Why not glasses? In our culture men wearing glasses, John claims, are perceived as having a weakness. Hal and Charlie aren't sure if he's right, but no one's ever figured out that bespectacled Clark Kent is Superman.

Grooming

Grooming is as serious a matter to the PI as the right clothes. Between the close contact of personal interviews and being constantly on the go, John finds he sweats a lot. Showers and deodorant become almost as important as TV commercials make them out to be. A shave every morning and even removing the five o'clock shadow before an evening interview give the impression of someone paying careful attention to detail. How would you feel if you were hiring a detective for an extremely sensitive matter and she showed up with a tangled mass of hair, smeared lipstick, an avalanche of white flakes on her dark jacket, mud caked on her huaraches, and enough perfume to pass for a prostitute?

For male PIs, well-groomed hair is just as important as for women. Regardless of what the general public accepts in hair styles and length, the PI has to pay careful attention. Yes, athletes, rock stars, kids and actors can get away with wild do's, shoulder-length, pony-tailed hair, and their initials cut into the side. The investigator has to deal with two segments of the population that are more traditionally oriented. Police regulations usually demand short hair, and even though younger officers wear it longer, it's still neat and clean-cut. Besides, the real people in the police power structure, those who can really help the PI, most often come from a generation that wants hair above the collar and wants to see the ears. Picture a PI in buckskins and braids walking into a small-town sheriff's office and wanting help in finding a local. The only aid he's likely to receive is out the door. The same is true in the courtroom. Do you think Billy Buckskin is going to be perceived as credible by the jury or Judge Straight?

Summary

Detectives are not fashion models, but they need to be conscious of their clothing and grooming to control the impression they create. That image might not be right, but, as Walter Cronkite used to say, that's the way it is. Power PIing.

Hints

1. If you were to clip out pictures of real PIs from dust covers, newspapers and magazines, you'd find a wide variety of dress. Josiah Thompson is usually captured in a black leather jacket; Fay Faron, in a hat and shapeless jacket; and Marilyn Greene, in a turtleneck. Jules Kroll, Ed Pankau and William Callahan

prefer the suit. Your PI will tend to mirror your own personal clothing tastes. However, you ought to have this PI dress appropriately for the particular situation called for in the case. Three-piece suits are nice for meeting CEOs, but not for tracking lost children across the Mojave.

2. We know a mystery writer who builds a wardrobe for her detective by snipping clothing out of catalogs and magazines. Writing descriptions of her PI in action then becomes an adult version of playing paper dolls.

WEAPONS

*Noon. The perfect time to pay a social call on Louis Vee's boss, Mr.
Euripedes. I slid the bookcase aside to reveal a personal arsenal that
could have armed the local National Guard. I had to make a show of
force, but I didn't want Mr. E. to feel I was overestimating him. I packed
light. Ankle gun — a .22 Baby Browning automatic. Malaysian throwing
dagger up the left sleeve. A .45 Goldcup automatic in the small of my
back. A 9mm Sig Sauer in my shoulder rig. The piece of resistance was
an SPAS Model 12, a sawed-off pump with pistol grip, extended
magazine, and laser-sighted, of course, that hung in a concealed pocket
of my trenchcoat.*

Richard Steele,
Josh Shepherd, PI

Almost every fictional investigator carries a piece. In fact, some
detectives are named for a weapon — Peter Gunn, Thomas Magnum,
Mike Hammer, Cannon, Remington Steele, Shell Scott, Colt Seav-
ers, and it's impossible to think of Dirty Harry Callahan without
seeing a .44 Magnum.

To Carry or Not to Carry

However, as this book concerns the real-life PI, only one question
here is really important: Does the average investigator carry a
weapon? Again, the best answer lies in the type of PI work done. In
large city firms where the detective performs computer searches,
does white-collar background research, reads through court records,
or even takes lunch at La Maisonette, a weapon is probably not
needed. And fictional detectives working the English country man-
sion scene rarely need a weapon to combat the quirky nephew who
poisons his eccentric rich aunt in the book closet.

But what about the real world, the detective who frequents that part of town Raymond Chandler refers to as those "mean streets"? In so much mystery fiction today, PIs who work this side of town continually run into penny-ante thugs, murderers and drug dealers, and they don't pack a gun or even a knife. How believable is it that a PI would enter the Down & Dirty Bar and Grill looking for a wife-beater and be armed only with his disarming wit and sharp tongue? In fiction, too often such a confrontation results in an exciting fistfight in which despite overwhelming odds, an array of exotic weapons, and a barrage of chairs and broken bottles, the hero emerges victorious, usually unscathed, never sore. As previously mentioned, in one of the recent Parker novels, a group of large males comes by Spenser's office to harass him. Spenser literally ties one hand behind his back and, after telling them what he will do, proceeds to pummel them all.

Why Carry

John points out that such scenes make for gripping action, but don't ring true. In real life, if Chuck Norris entered the Down & Dirty Bar and Grill unarmed, he'd end up un-alive. And if Steven Seagal or even Josh Shepherd tried beating up the Neanderthal Mob in his office, he'd end up bagged—with a tag on his toe. Fistfights are for high school kids, and nobody in the real world cares how loud you scream "Uncle!" Remember the noseguard for the San Diego Chargers who thought his well-developed musculature gave him an advantage in a macho bar? He was out of pro football for a year doing rehab. In the real world, then, there's no such thing as a fair fight. Everybody fights to win, whatever it takes. Disability, maiming and killing are the goals. Weapons are the keys to victory.

John recalls wandering into a bar in downtown Atlanta after successfully finding, capturing and turning over a fugitive. While John was celebrating, a local tough guy pointed out that John was sitting on his bar stool. John stood up and gave it to him. The man glared. Recognizing the danger signs, John said he was leaving and that the man could have the whole bar. The man picked up John and began to headbutt him. John reached into the small of his back, pulled out a .38 and used it as a tongue depressor. Then he assured his assailant he had no qualms about blowing away someone he didn't know or care about. The man let him depart. Without the .38, though, and through no fault of his own, John would have been badly injured at best.

The hard truth is that in so many investigations, the PI, especially the small-town version or the one-person op in the big city, is forced to go into situations where he's not wanted, places where he doesn't fit and where the Neanderthal code — survival of the fittest — is the law of the land. If your PI carries a gun, s/he should wear it from page one. In some PI fiction the detective finally straps on a weapon at the climax because danger definitely lurks ahead. In real life, a detective never knows when the need will arise.

Nonetheless, some real-life PIs who stalk the mean streets refuse to carry a weapon. Book-writing gumshoe Josiah Thompson operates in San Francisco. Partially because he was once a professor of philosophy at a prestigious liberal arts school, he doesn't carry a gun. He thinks a gun gives the wearer a false sense of confidence, and it also means stooping to the level of gun-toting criminals. And statistics show that even most beat cops never fire their weapons. Still, they all carry a few, and almost all will at one time or another draw and point.

One reason Ed Hino left the FBI was to get away from the gun. Too many friends got killed, and one day he found himself asking if he wanted to be a target. Still, he walked into a Pennsylvania sheriff's office, filed the necessary forms, got himself fingerprinted, swore he had never been convicted of a crime, and was issued a permit to carry a concealed weapon.

Does John carry a gun? At all times. In fact, he usually carries two: a .38 Smith & Wesson clipped on to his belt and a .25 pistol stuck into what looks like a wallet in his back pocket. He also has been known to carry a derringer-size revolver in his belt, another on his ankle, and even one that fits into a device that looks like a pocket beeper. While John doesn't walk around in Kevlar suits weighted down for action, he is ready. His car contains, among other things (to be discussed in the next chapter) automatic weapons, and in his home he has enough hardware to stock a gun store. But John admits that a PI doesn't have to own this much hardware — the fact of the matter is that he likes guns.

Why does John pack? Very simply, he believes it's better to have a weapon and not need it than to need it and not have it. He likes to quote the old eastern Kentucky sheriff who once told him, "I'd rather be tried by twelve [the number of bullets in a clip] than carried by six [pallbearers]." And, guns don't have to be fired to be effective.

Rotten Apple—The Cowboy

Cowboys live in a world of their own. They rarely follow normal legal and moral guidelines for investigations, whether they're eavesdropping, illegally searching and seizing, or failing to maintain the chain of evidence. In fact, they usually exhibit a total disdain for the law and are willing to use any means to achieve their ends.

The cowboy's actions create an atmosphere of endangerment—for the client, missing persons the PI locates and tries to extricate, even bystanders. Cowboys tend to favor weapons over brainpower. Their clients can become parties to their crimes and possibly liable for damages. Legitimate PIs and smart clients shy away from them, although some clients have problems/cases so bizarre that only a cowboy will touch them.

Research the Weapon

If you have your PI carry a weapon, get the information right. People who read PI fiction often care a great deal about weapons. They can forgive Tom Clancy if he tells us (as he does in his latest novel) that Tommy Nobis played middle linebacker for the University of Alabama against Texas (it was the other way around), but should Clancy launch a nuclear rocket from the wrong size tube, they toss his book like a live grenade. To some extent this reaction is justified. Readers running into revolvers with safeties can assume they know more than the writer. John loves Loren Estleman and has long considered Amos Walker to be among the most realistic detectives. However, in a recent novel about gunrunning, when the Detroit detective let the hammer down on a German Luger, John had to gag. *Lugers don't have hammers.*

A pistol may not be enough. Detectives working in rural areas may come up against rifles with scopes. Detectives in cities, like cops, are apt to run into automatic weapons. Therefore, you have to arm your PI appropriately.

We don't have the space to suggest what your PI should carry. Besides, the first book of the Howdunit series, *Armed and Dangerous*, by Michael Newton is a good source. Read his book and talk to a local gunsmith. Even a town the size of Richmond, Kentucky (population 23,000), has three gun shops, and the people in each are happy to discuss guns and provide interesting information. Research weaponry, for if you choose to have your PI use a gun, you want to be as accurate as Mike Hammer when he fires. Any supermarket shelf is crowded with gun magazines with straightforward titles like *Guns & Ammo* and *Handguns for Sport & Defense*. Bookstores have sections devoted to weapons from the most common handgun to exotic Ninja instruments of death.

A Visit to the Gun Shop

If you're one of those people who cringe at the sound of gunfire, won't watch Dirty Harry movies, and wouldn't accept an N(a-tional) R(ifle) A(ssociation) membership as a gift, yet need to know about firearms for your story, the easiest way to locate the information is to visit a local gun shop.

What do you do there? Start by following the "10 Tips 4 Interviewers" (page 14). In addition, you might ask some of the following questions:

- What weapon would you advise the average citizen to carry? (Several shopkeepers suggested to us the S&W .38 Chief with the two-inch barrel.)

- If I were creating a PI to live in _____, what would be a likely weapon to carry? (Specify the place and gender of your PI. Most shopkeepers told us a 9mm automatic; .45 is big; .40 is newer; go for high capacity—16 shots, or as one gunsmith put it, "In a tight situation, would you rather have five shots, or fifteen in the clip and one in the chamber?")

- What local, state and federal regulations must I be aware of? (Most gun shops can tell you laws; many, in fact, post regulations.)

- Are there any accessories I should be aware of? (Shops usually carry catalogs for holsters and other equipment such as speed-loaders.)

■ Is the gun safe? (Most handguns today are manufactured with a transfer bar safety; they can't go off until the weapon is cocked.)

Know the Laws

If you have your PI carry a weapon, be sure, too, to check the laws of your detective's state. As we pointed out in chapter three, state laws differ greatly. Some states have differing licenses for those who carry and those who don't (again, check the status of your state). In Ohio, for instance, no class A, B or C licensee (or employee thereof) can carry a firearm without: 1) successfully completing a basic firearms training program, 2) submitting an application requesting permission to carry, and 3) receiving notification on an identification card of being a firearms bearer. In Florida, class C and D licensees are permitted to carry firearms if they apply for a class G license, which authorizes statewide use of a gun, but that gun may not be concealed. To get that class G license, a detective must have eight to ten hours of range and classroom training, as well as a clean police record and general good character. Finally, a Florida-based PI can carry only "a standard police .38 caliber revolver with standard ammunition" unless otherwise authorized by the state.

As with licensing, the easiest way to find out these regulations is simply to ask your local police or sheriff. We found that the one subject about which cops are unanimously knowledgeable and eager to discuss is guns.

John's work often calls for him to be out of state, so he has to know these laws. At home he feels comfortable with his snub-nosed Colt Cobra. With its shrouded hammer so that it won't snag, the airweight .38 is a good "dress-up gun." But is it legal in Indiana? Can he transport his wallet-sized Walther PPK with him? John always checks. But, truthfully, one rule PIs often follow is: "If you want it, you better bring it in." Some states have waiting periods to obtain guns, while others make it illegal for nonresidents to purchase weapons.

Summary

John is no cowboy, and despite one of his business cards, his gun is not for hire. Although he's been offered both, he won't marry or murder for money. Nonetheless, he is well over twenty-one, operates in the very real world, handles many cases a year, and ends up having to go where violence is as much a part of everyday life as breathing. In more than twenty-one years in the business, he's been involved in only six fights, but twenty shootings. Still, John suggests, there are better weapons than those measured by calibers. One is money. John has bought information with a fifty-dollar bill that he couldn't have scared out with a Thompson submachine gun. And he does have one (guns and bills).

And the number-one, can't-fail, 100 percent, surefire weapon in the investigator's arsenal? For John, sex. But that's the subject of a later chapter.

Oh, yeah, Richard Steele better double-check Josh's Baby Browning. It's a .25 caliber, not a .22.

Hints

1. Remember to research the guns your bad guys carry, too. With the availability of Saturday night specials and automatic weapons, zip guns are pretty much out.

2. Check the police also. Interestingly, both crooks and cops carry "hideout" guns (hidden), and the .38 snub-nose is fairly common for the job. In their holsters now, cops are switching to the 9mm because it can get off more shots and is easier to load.

3. A relevant pamphlet: Schlesinger, Henry. *Federal Gun Laws.* n.p.: n.p., 1989. This book covers such things as definitions of firearms and ammunition; laws pertaining to the transfer of firearms and ammo; unlawful interstate shipment of arms; importation/exportation of arms; registration thereof; taxes; firearms aboard aircraft; postal regulations pertaining to firearms; possession of firearms in national parks and forests; licenses to produce, sell, import/export firearms; and penalties for breaking federal laws pertaining to these matters.

   Schlesinger also provides some interesting graphics of illegal firearms.

   Again, a caveat, but this time from the author: "Although the information contained herein has been obtained from sources believed to be reliable, the author does not guarantee same, nor assume any responsibility for the interpretations of the laws . . . To determine the applicability of these laws to specific situations which you may encounter, you are strongly urged to consult a local attorney or the government agency charged with their administration."

4. If you wonder if you need any special research on guns, take this elementary quiz.
   A. Do ankle rigs come in different sizes? Right- and left-handed carry? Can they be adjusted for cant and height?
   B. Can laser-aim and telescopic sights be mounted on handguns?
   C. Why are Smith & Wesson Centennial and J-frame Bodyguard models especially appropriate for concealed carry?
   D. Can single-action and double-action revolvers be customized so as to lessen their trigger pulls?
   E. What feature on a semi-auto most presents problems to a left-handed shooter?
   F. What is a major disadvantage of a "fanny pack" holster?
   G. For best results even at close range, at what level should a handgun be fired?
   H. What handgun is most often used by criminals?
   I. Of the eighteen top handguns used by criminals, are the majority semi-autos or revolvers?
   J. What percentage of guns used in violent crimes are traced?
   Answers: A) Yes, B) Yes, C) They're hammerless, D) Yes, E) The safety catch, F) Slow to draw and they bounce against the body, G) Shoulder height, H) .38/.357 Smith & Wesson, I) Semi-autos, J) 1 percent.

5. Chekhov advised young writers never to introduce a gun into a play unless they intended to have it fired. We suggest the Chekhovian Corollary: Never place a weapon in your fiction unless you have thoroughly researched that weapon.

6. Familiarize yourself with gun laws—local, state and federal. Most people, for instance, believe that the Constitutional right to bear arms grants unrestricted privilege to anybody. Wrong.
   Can your gun-toting PI cross a county or state line without violating various laws? Yes and no. If your PI carries the .38 in a shoulder rig beneath a jacket, every county line crossed is another law broken. But if your PI stores the .38 unloaded in

the trunk, s/he can journey from point Alpha to point Omega without breaking the law courtesy of the little-known Federal Firearm Owners Protection Act (FOPA) of 1986.

Can your detective store a loaded 9mm in the Ford's glove compartment legally? Only in Kentucky. Of the fifty states, at the moment only this middle-America commonwealth doesn't classify the glove box as a place of concealment. Under the coat, however, is illegal. Your PI could stride down Main Street anywhere in Kentucky with .45's in a double holster a la Wyatt Earp and not violate the law.

The only people who can carry a concealed weapon? Duly authorized law enforcement officials. Kentucky even has a law that municipalities can't enact restrictions on gun purchasing any more restrictive than federal provisions.

As a shortcut to looking up the various states' laws, you could consult an annual publication of the Bureau of Alcohol, Tobacco and Firearms, *ATF P 5300.5* (Information Programs, 1200 Pennsylvania Avenue NW, Washington, D.C. 20226). It contains state firearms laws and local ordinances as well as listing federal restrictions.

7. Want your PI to be The Kevlar Kid? For a catalog on body armor, contact Safariland for their ordering guide (3120 E. Mission Boulevard, Ontario, California 91761; 1-800-347-1200).

EQUIPMENT

Lightly armed, I turned to loading the trunk of the Green Monster, the car I drove when the Ferrari was in the shop. Which seemed more often than a client walked through the door. First, I packed my disguise kit, complete with makeup, wigs and beards. I put the fingerprint kit in next followed by the portable polygraph. Then the camcorder, the backup tape recorder, the strobe and the gas-powered generator. For good measure I tossed in the TASER, the new Nikon with telescopic lens and the long-distance microphone. On top I piled my briefcase of business cards and my portable printing press in case I needed something new.

Richard Steele,
Josh Shepherd, PI

Obviously Josh Shepherd was once a successful Boy Scout and since has been prepared to the max, but how much investigative equipment does the detective need? While some of the large agencies own all sorts of sophisticated electronic gear for counterespionage, surveillance and even computer data searches, the average PI gets by with a lot less—some of it low tech, some of it no tech.

Even so, times have changed since the game was afoot and Sherlock Holmes stalked his quarry aided only by his trusty magnifying glass. While the *L.L. Shamus Catalogue* stocks a myriad of gadgets that could be used, the average PI starting out doesn't need a lot of money or a long order form. And some equipment is more important than others once the PI leaves the office.

Car

Absolutely indispensable. Well running preferred to late model. High performance engine not necessary, but more than basic power is. Not high profile. Common brand. Fairly common colors. Earth tones preferable to citrus colors. Resembling the Feds can be a plus and a negative, depending on whether you're trying to impress a client/interviewee or not stand out in a surveillance. Car phone more and more valuable.

Pencil and Paper

As it was in the beginning and still is today, a good PI doesn't hit the streets without a pad of paper/notebook and several writing instruments handy. TV, fiction and the movies too often portray the PI as a disciple of Harry Lorayne, the memory expert. Such detectives see a license plate one time or overhear a phone number once, and amidst the clutter and minutiae of everyday life, they don't forget the information. You know, "February 6, 1976, about 7:30 in the evening? Yeah, I remember exactly what I was doing . . ." John points out that in the course of a day he works several cases and is deluged with detail. People provide information, he observes things and occasionally a brainstorm occurs. He must be able to jot down these things so that he can later study them.

Tape Recorder

A medium tech version of the notepad, the recorder is John's preference. Instead of approximating what witnesses say with his pencil, he can record it verbatim. Later he can play it back and listen for word choice, inflection, tone, what wasn't said. And he has a greater degree of certainty. Moreover, as he has to occasionally go to court, John finds this accuracy essential. Recorders are cheap, easy to handle and free his hands. When he writes, John, like most of us, finds he looks down, and in an interview making eye contact and observing physical mannerisms are extremely important. In surveillance, often he can't afford to take his eyes off the subject to jot down something, and when he drives, he finds it easier and safer to record his thoughts on tape. Audiotapes are cheap and permanent records easily established. One caveat: John learned long ago the necessity of carrying backup batteries.

Dressed to Kill—Not!

Writers bulletproof their manuscripts; PIs protect themselves physically. As a result of the latter, the self-protection business is booming. American Body Armor & Equipment Inc. of Florida reports its revenue rose 35 percent for the first three quarters of 1991; operating revenue in 1990 was $13 million. Guardian Group International is running 25 percent ahead of the previous year.

Why? Crime in general and robberies in particular are growth industries.

So what's the well-protected PI wearing these days?

How about a Kevlar-lined raincoat that will stop a 9mm slug? A mere $1,200 from Guardian. They also have a $2,200 umbrella that keeps out rain and rooftop snipers. Bargain-hunting? A $325 bulletproof clipboard might help.

Camcorder

One step up the technical ladder is the camcorder. Obviously it has all the advantages of the tape recorder plus visuals. While it might not be effective for a simple interview (many people clam up with a camera in their face or at least become more nervous), the camcorder can be used in surveillance work, recording a crime scene for exact detail and security. Now that the price has dropped to around $500, it certainly falls within the budget of most PIs.

On the other hand, Terry Lasky, a New York City investigator, prefers to shoot with a $12,000 8-millimeter TV news camera equipped with a 16-to-1 zoom lens.

Camera

One popular image of the PI has him poking his Polaroid through a peephole to photograph Cheating Bob, the philandering husband rendezvousing at the Hot Sheet Motel with the other women while playing in the background is "Let's tryst again like we did last summer." The PI's camera has other functions. Sometimes the detective wants a file photo, and a picture of a runaway is easier to show the parents for a positive I.D. Cameras can get into places camcorders can't, and telephoto lens can easily be attached to cameras. John suggests a simple autofocus model is best so the detective can shoot fast. Also, to be sure he's got the shot, John defends the Polaroid. He knows right away what has developed.

Some PIs also own infrared cameras and keep high-speed film around to shoot in the dark. Ed Hino finds a Canon AE-1 sufficient. He has discovered, too, that in court he can be just as good a witness as a picture.

Binoculars

They cost so little, but see so much. They're standard operating procedure for much surveillance. The more high-powered, the better. The smaller size is preferred for concealment and ease of carrying. Besides, what detective wants to look like General Patton observing the troops and call attention to himself?

Sunglasses

Much surveillance takes place outside, and glare definitely obscures vision, especially for blue-eyed investigators. Moreover, when the detective wears particularly dark shades, it's difficult for people to tell exactly what's being looked at (though it makes a male look like a Blues Brother or a Fed). Obviously, no PI wants to advertise to suspects they're under surveillance. Eye contact is definitely something the PI wishes to avoid. Sunglasses also notably change the wearer's look, thus becoming one of the simplest, easiest forms of disguise. Therefore, it's important the PI not wear a flashy pair that stands out.

Hats

They work like sunglasses in keeping the glare out and making another simple disguise. John keeps a collection, often lying on the backseat of his car. One way he blends in locally is by removing his coat and tie, then donning a baseball cap (Pride in tobacco and the Cincinnati Reds are area favorites). Bogie is dead; the fedora, out. John even owns two hats that have ponytails attached.

Beeper/Cellular Phone

John began with a beeper, advanced to a car phone, and now has a portable cellular phone he places on the table in McDonald's next to his coffee. During the last few years the cost of such phones has dropped dramatically, and service has become available in most areas. It's almost a necessity for the detective to be able to make contact or be contacted any time, any place. Since PIs spend so much time driving, the phone allows them flexibility. While traveling to see a client, a detective can check a source, make an appointment and even do research. John likes the sense of security they provide. If somebody has to absolutely, positively get in touch with him, they can. Beepers work, but they provide a lot of lag time, and beepers go off at the wrong time, calling unwanted attention to PIs. They forget, too, that they have them on.

Flashlight

Two will do—with backup batteries. A small light can be carried in the PI's coat pocket, and a large light not only shines brightly but doubles as a weapon (it looks innocent, but makes a nice billy club). Often on surveillance John uses the small light to read documents, for unlike the car's dome light it doesn't call attention to him or drain his battery. Also, John doesn't work a nine-to-five job, and a lot of picking around crime scenes is done at night. Some flashlights even have a built-in tear gas or Mace sprayer.

Electronics

Bugs, sweepers, long-distance parabolic and directional microphones and the like all work, but aren't needed very often and cost a lot. Of course, phone-bugs/wiretapping is illegal. Because there is a good market for debugging, specialty firms most often use these expensive devices to detect bugs, but the average PI is more concerned with cockroaches.

Multipurpose Knife

Most investigators can't find as many uses for the venerable Swiss Army knife as MacGyver, but a good utility knife is indispensable.

John recalls numerous times he has had to unscrew a panel, scrape rust from metal, cut a rope, clip off deadly hangnails, or perform some other act that is simple with the right tool; a nightmare without it. Sometimes John has been known to slit the tires of suspects to delay them.

Fingerprint Kit

Although a kit to lift fingerprints sounds at worst like Dick Tracy's Junior Crimebusters or the province of the police, at times the PI can use it. Usually, though, a PI doesn't investigate the crime scene, so the kit isn't really necessary. When he first started, John bought a kit. In all his years he's used it twice. Once, though, he lifted the palm print of a convenience store murderer, so the kit paid for itself.

The Most Important Piece of Field Equipment

A wide-mouthed bottle. Surveillances often demand a fixed position, and a detective can't always leave to heed the call of nature. Most experienced PIs also use a cap.

Four Can't-Do-Without, Indispensible, Gotta-Have-It Catalogs

1. *Police Equipment*
   P.O. Box 882
   New York, New York 10150
   Like other Henry Schlesinger material, this book is hopelessly out of date. The author sells hardcore police gear, but has marked up each price in handwriting. Probably not state-of-the-art in catalogs or equipment, the book contains fingerprint kits, crime detection kits, holsters, ultraviolet equipment, leather goods, lock pick equipment (not sold to just anybody) and police armor.
2. *Things You Never Knew Existed*
   Johnson C. Smith Co.
   4514 19th Street Court East
   P.O. Box 25500
   Bradenton, Florida 34206-5500
   Your suspicions that this may be only a novelty catalog are

first aroused by the name of the company (the same pseudonym Stephen Crane used to publish *Maggie* in 1890), which consists of the two most popular names in the phone book. Private eyes will find numerous uses for phony dog poop (possibly to hide a spare set of keys outdoors), a *police* baseball cap (which might just show support for your favorite rock group), a concealed leather shoulder holster, a telephone tap detector, the powerful bionic ear (costing less than $6 million) and a counterfeit bill detector.

3. *Guns & Ammo.*

This magazine has a classified ads section that lists numerous gun catalogs, assault weapons accessories, conversion kits, repliguns, collectibles, specialized targets (e.g., Saddam Hussein or your mother-in-law) and espionage apparati.

4. Paladin Press
   P.O. Box 1307
   Boulder, Colorado 80306

You say you've always wanted to learn the secrets of Oriental fighting techniques that were old when the world was young? You hate your spouse? You want revenge on your fatuous brother-in-law for all those practical jokes he pulls? Seriously, if it's something dastardly you'd like to inquire into, this company probably publishes a book on it. Want revenge? Buy *Kickass.* Learn how to obtain a new I.D. Cook up some foul dish in the *Anarachist Cookbook.* Attend *PI School.* See how to perform illegal telephone taps. Ever want to be a *Hit Man*? Need the skinny on *Ninja Mind Control* (they got our attention)? Care about weapons, surveillance, videos, military science, or Special Forces survival training? You've read *What Color Is Your Parachute?* and want to switch careers. Paladin has a book on the splendid opportunities available in gunrunning. Ah, you've had your eye on sniping (vs. common, everyday snipping) for some time. They've even got the word for the next generation's Benjamin Braddocks—"homemade silencers."

Geronimo!

How to Get Them

Obviously most of the no-tech devices—hats, shades, bottles, flashlights—are available at the local Kmart. For high tech equipment the PI usually has to visit law enforcement supply houses, which exist in most large cities and can be located in the Yellow Pages. Some PIs, John says, visit national trade shows and conventions, though often the locale is a greater drawing card than the latest high tech hardware. Another good source of such equipment is the mail-order catalog of electronic emporiums like The Sharper Image, Hammacher Schlemmer, DAK and Damark.

Summary

Two factors determine the PI's equipment inventory: specialty and budget. And often the latter determines the former.

Hints

1. Technology changes so fast that it is impossible to keep up. What's new when you write your book can be superannuated by the time it appears in the stores.

2. Two excellent sources for high tech equipment in the security industry are the newest editions of the *Security Letter Source-Book* (New York: Security Letter) and Bell Atlantic's *Security Industry* (Bethesda: C&P Telephone of Virginia). These books detail alarm systems, access control, locks, communication equipment and surveillance devices.

3. If you can't find either of these books or a police supply house in your area, you might try ordering some relevant catalogs. Five of the most well-known are:
   - *Hammacher Schlemmer* (800) 421-9002
   - *The Sharper Image* (800) 344-5555
   - *DAK* (800) DAK-0800
     8200 Remmet Avenue
     Canoga Park, California 91304
   - *DAMARK* (800) 729-9000
     7101 Winnetka Avenue North
     P.O. Box 29900
     Minneapolis, Minnesota 55429-0900
   - *Heartland America* (800) 229-2901
     6978 Shady Oak Road
     Eden Prairie, Minnesota 55344-3453

Other catalogs are much more specialized and not sent to the general public.

Can't wait? Try shopping at your local electronics store, though one prominent national company reputedly has a policy of not selling to customers their salespeople suspect might use the equipment illegally (it makes you wonder how they determine such a thing).

What kind of gadgetry is available? Everything from surveillance microphones and cameras to an X-ray spray that turns paper translucent for a minute (a real bargain at $25, especially if you're worried about your enemies sending you letter bombs). A foldup umbrella costs $300, but it not only keeps off the rain, it allows you to eavesdrop long-distance.

Here's a brief survey of handy hardware for the contemporary Sam Spade.

- The Audio Telescope: a super-directional shotgun mike, seventeen inches long, twenty-foot mike cable. You can "pick a voice out of a crowd or a sparrow's song out of a tree." DAK ($49.90).
- Portable Voice-Stress Analyzer: a portable lie detector. Sophisticated models can be connected to a tape recorder and have printout capabilities. Communication Control System Ltd. ($3,000-$12,000).
- Secret Connection Attache Case: briefcase with secreted tape recorder. Will accept wiretap alerts, scramblers, night vision devices. Communication Control System Ltd. ($500-$15,000).
- Infinity Transmitter: picks up conversations within a thirty-foot radius. Transmits data directly over phone lines. Can be concealed anywhere. Criminal Research Products Inc. ($600).
- Telephone Recorder: automatically records conversation each time the handset is picked up. Life Force Technologies Ltd. ($500).
- Veritrac 9000: voice-activated taping system that can record 240 conversations simultaneously. Dictaphone Corp. ($10,000-$12,000).
- Bearcat BC200XLT: a police scanner that picks up police and fire communications between 800 and 900 megahertz. Cellular frequencies omitted at factory, but can

easily be modified to listen in on cellular calls. Bearcat ($259).

- NT-1 Scoopman: tiny digital tape recorder the size of a postage stamp that stores two hours of tape. Weighs 5.2 ounces. Sony ($800).
- Ground Penetrating Radar-Infrared Overflight: contact Strategic Air Command. Not all customers qualify. Rates inflated to keep pace with latest Pentagon buying habits.
- Investigators On-Line: a computer network run by Ralph Thomas's Datafax Information Services of Austin, Texas. Provides PIs, lawyers and corporate clients access to many data banks. Capable of locating skips, missing witnesses or relatives, untangling computer frauds or screening potential corporate execs.
- Caller I.D. Prescreening of the number of every incoming call. Available in about half the states; banned in others. Hooks directly to telephone. Monthly charge (less than $10) plus equipment cost (about $75). Basic electronic screen available from Sears.
- Micro Bugs. For a catalog of new-wave bugging equipment, write Microcom Technology, Dept. M, P.O. Box 347341, Cleveland, Ohio 44134.
- Beecher Mirage Binoculars. Pair of 7×30 binoculars worn like eyeglasses. Uses eight 1mm-thick mirrors and fourteen multicolored lenses.
- Viewing Scope. 3¼×3×1½. Weighs two ounces. Fully coated optics with fingertip control. Edmund Scientific Company, Dept. 2102, Y2, Edscorp Building, Barrington, New York 08007 ($34.95).
- Night Surveillance System (NSS). Radio-controlled miniature submarine with periscope, low-light video camera, radio data-link that can transmit images in the dark of night. Contact Perry Offshore, Inc. of Riviera Beach, Florida.

4. Edmund Scientific Company (101 E. Glouchester Pike, Barrington, New Jersey 08007-1380; 609-547-8880) offers a range of binoculars including a Spy Scope (305-foot field of view at 1,000 yards; two ounces), an Electronic Datascope, magnifying glass and microscopes.

INITIATING CLIENT RELATIONSHIPS

Halfway to Euripedes's sanctum sanctorum, I got an emergency call on my cellular phone from an old friend, insisting we meet. I picked the Glass Garden, a popular eaterie, then called ahead to reserve a power table near the entrance. When Carolyn showed at 1:00, I greeted her loudly and embraced her warmly. The rubberneckers probably thought we were engaged. The whole meal boiled down to cabbage au gratin and my assurance that I'd work on her case exclusively. My heart and soul were in this one, and I'd get her money back. Josh Shepherd only went one way, I assured her, all the way.

Richard Steele,
Josh Shepherd, PI

An executive in the hotel business once described the key to success in his field as the number of "heads in beds." To some extent a detective depends on an adequate caseload. It's not so much the sheer number of clients, though, as much as having a steady flow of paying customers, especially in cases with a high profit margin.

PIs agree that the most difficult part of any case is not the time and money spent or even playing between the fair poles. It's dealing with the person who hires them—establishing, maintaining, controlling and closing the relationship with the client. In fact, one detective puts it bluntly: "You expect everybody to lie to you, especially your client."

Contact

Throughout this book, we've stressed that private investigation is a business, but when it comes to clients, it's often conducted differently from other businesses. If you were selling widgets, you would contact people, send your sales force out to alert them to the wondrous world of widgets, and customers would drop by your office. But with PIs it's a different ball game. PIs do little selling of themselves, almost never go looking for a client, don't have an army of salespeople or P.R. flacks, and clients rarely crack the door to see if THE DETECTIVE IS IN sign is up.

As with most small firms, the majority of John's initial contacts are by phone. Hardly ever has he been initially approached in a public place by a prospective client (except attorneys, who will talk shop even during church and funerals). Rarely has anyone just happened by his office or home, and in all the years only once did a request come by mail. Yet in hard-boiled detective stories from Spade to Spenser the client shows up from nowhere ("She appeared in my office like she'd been conjured up by Satan himself"). Large firms, of course, operate more like a traditional business. Some are actually on retainer, some have ongoing contracts with a large client base, and most receive requests by all methods — by phone, in person and via fax.

Initial Meeting

No matter how contact is made, John finds his clients prefer their first face-to-face to be outside of the office (though occasionally some are brought by his office and coached by women friends). Most people needing a detective are nervous about it, and they desire a high degree of secrecy. They don't want a friend or neighbor to spot them walking into Josh Shepherd's office.

Therefore, public places, especially restaurants, are preferred. The detective and client don't stand out — they're just two friends having lunch. Being in public, the client also feels a degree of security. The very fact they need a detective is an admission of vulnerability, so comfort matters more psychologically. Most people, too, don't see a detective the way they do a doctor — it's usually a one-time proposition and one without a guidebook. With all the conflicting media images of the PI, they don't know what to expect. Eating out in our culture is absolute normalcy. It's a commonplace domestic situation that John finds women clients feel especially comfortable about.

John will never forget one initial meeting where the client took anonymity to the extreme. His client, a local blonde who everybody in the community, including John, knew by sight, set up the meet. First she picked Lexington, a large city twenty-five minutes to the north. Then she chose a popular pickup bar where members of the opposite sex seen conversing was de rigueur. It was a 4:00 appointment. By 4:30 the client still hadn't shown, but a long-haired brunette was glancing at John through the smoke-filled darkness. By 5:00 the brunette was winking, and the blonde client still hadn't appeared. A few minutes later a drink arrived for John, which the waiter explained was from the brunette. Deciding his client was a no-show, John walked over to thank the brunette and to explain he was working. She took him aside and whispered, "It's me, you fool," then explained she was wearing a disguise.

Client Assessment

Very quickly during the initial meeting—which costs the detective time and the client nothing—the detective must size up the client and the potential case to determine whether or not to take it. Many factors affect the decision.

In movies and TV the detective accepts every case. In real life, the detective turns people down for a host of reasons. In TV the detective's major reason for taking the case is usually emotional involvement—a family member, an old fishing buddy, a lover. Occasionally the fictional PI is overwhelmed by the unquestionable righteousness of the client's problem—the ex-spouse has kidnapped their child, a famed con man has taken their money, or "Somebody is framing me." In real life, the very fact that there even could be emotional involvement often precludes the detective from taking the case.

As previously mentioned, one of John's Ten Commandments is *Thou Shall Not Become Involved With Thy Client*. Why? Because when he loses his objectivity, John finds he makes other bad judgments.

So what considerations does the PI take?

Ability to pay: In movies and TV the client is often poor, but what happens? Have you ever seen a show where the PI says, "Although I think you have been wronged by the Mob/your ex/the law's indifference, I'm turning you down because you can't afford me"? In real life, a detective makes a living investigating, and since there's little repeat business except for corporations and law firms, freebies are not a sound business practice. The client's ability to pay upon the PI's completion of the job, not in ten monthly installments, is an important factor. John and other PIs have turned people down because a credit reference bureau has labelled them a bad risk. John even knows one person in the PI biz whose motto is "All my clients are considered innocent until proven – broke."

Would a client ever really stiff a detective, a person whose lifeblood is tracking down such people? Yes. Once John even got a bad personal check from a member of the CIA, and in a matter of pride John just had to go to our nation's capital to get his money. But that's another story.

Mental state: Another crucial factor is psychological stability. If a client comes to John with a tale that his wife has been kidnapped and he's been told to take the ransom payment to the bridge over the creek, and wait for the UFO, John obviously hesitates. The clincher for John in one such case was that his client told him she had been instructed to bring the payment in small bundles of pine bark mulch. But not all instabilities are so obvious. Some people are chronic liars; others have an elaborate fantasy life. Some possess extreme phobias; some have a long-standing history of problems. This doesn't mean detectives like to discriminate against people with psychological aberrations. The PI is a trained investigator, not a professional counselor, though many clients seeking the former actually need the latter. Detectives try to avoid undesired personal relationships, for people with mental problems can fixate on the detective as an apparently stable authority figure. Such persons could pose a risk to the detective's friends and family, interfere in other investigations, and provide a plethora of legal problems.

However, some unscrupulous PIs (see the mine-salter, page 42) cultivate a clientele of the unstable and cater to their delusions, especially their fears. "Well, Mr. Screwloose, our crack investigative team has produced proof positive that someone big and powerful really is out there to get you by making you seem paranoid." The key is that Mr. Screwloose must be able to afford his delusions.

Character: Obviously, then, another critical factor is truth – is the client deliberately lying? John figures that 99 percent of his clients fail to tell the truth – some deliberately, some unintentionally. Some commit the lie; some lie by omission. In the initial interview, if he's considering the person across the table as a real client, John tries to learn as much as he can about the person — the personality as well as the hard facts. Are they responsible? Dependable? How long have they held their job? Been married a while? Moved frequently? Financially stable? And they may lie about these things too, so experience counts. John studies body language (see chapter fourteen), eye contact, voice inflection, hesitation and inconsistencies.

Goal: The detective also considers what the client wants. And there's often a vast difference between what clients say they want and what they really want. Sometimes that's a conscious difference; others, unconscious. For instance, one woman who hired John to do bodyguard work was really trying to set him up to kill her husband so she could marry her new boyfriend. Sometimes the story told to John is secondary; the client's primary desire is just to have someone to listen to them for an hour and then they disappear. Other would-be clients have the celebrity autograph syndrome. They simply want to be able to mention to their friends that they once dealt with a PI, and "Let me tell you, she's nothing like in the movies." Some are drowning in their own problems or are embarrassed (e.g., usually people jilted or conned). As a result, John spends a lot of time sorting through the baggage to find the Samsonite.

The Law: One question a PI always asks is: Can the police handle it? In TV and movies the PI often takes a homicide case. In real life, such investigations are best left to the various levels of police. Occasionally a lawyer might ask John to look into the case of someone accused of a crime — i.e., defense work. Sometimes a case has grown "stale" — the police have in effect closed the files — but some relative is not satisfied "They're doing all they can" and hires John to look into it. Usually, if a PI finds that the police *have* done all they can, the detective will not deliberately step on toes.

Legal problems: A PI will also assess the legality of the client's desires. Clients occasionally want the detective to attempt something illegal. John has been asked to terrorize an ex-boyfriend, break into a lawyer's office to steal divorce records, tap the work phone of a wife suspected of cheating, extort money from a business rival, even to make a key trial witness disappear. Given the state regulatory boards, the overlapping layers of law enforcement and the litigious climate of the country, a detective has to heed the advice of Hill Street Watch Sergeant Phil Esterhaus: "Be careful out there!"

Caseload: Detectives must know how much work they have going at any one time and how much they can reasonably handle. If the PI has a week of court testimony coming up, the need to fly to Albuquerque, a seminar in the kinesic method of interrogation, or even a son's Little League tournament, taking the case, no matter how appealing, may be undesirable. A PI's caseload is highly individualistic. At one extreme are TV detectives who appear to work only one job at a time; every waking hour is devoted to *The Big Case* with nary a mention of other work. At the other extreme are the small-town PIs who overload themselves. To paraphrase Will Rogers, they never met a case they didn't like. And like small-town contractors, they take every job that comes their way, start on it, fly to another worksite, and then finish the original job at their leisure. Part-time detectives have to be careful of their load. Working full-time as a college teacher, Ed Hino is painfully aware there are only twenty-four hours in a day, and with just two part-timers to count on, he must select only a few cases. And, of course, no matter how interesting the potential case seems, Hino will pass on it if it conflicts with his tee-time.

Money, Money, Money: Which brings up the joker in the deck. Some detectives will take on any case that comes their way because they need quick cash. Other PIs will try just one more straw. But money, or the absence of it, is a strong motivator. One night about 8:30 John got a phone call from a man living two-and-a-half hours away. The potential client was eager, pressuring John to drive up the next morning. John, tired and busy with a few ongoing investigations, was hesitant. The client mentioned a $5,000 retainer. John drove over that night.

Suitability: Occasionally detectives are offered an appealing, money-making case they'd really like to take, but if they're honest, they realize the case goes beyond their scope, abilities or expertise. Small-town PIs might be asked to perform high tech surveillance work or investigate computer fraud when they aren't capable. John, for instance, is an expert on firearms and people, but not the IBM PS/2 system or the Prodigy network. Somebody whose house burned down might want a trained arson investigator, but that's not the PI's specialty. Location is very important. Getting away from the home territory makes the PI a fish out of water. John, for instance, after an unfortunate incident south of the border, wouldn't take a case under any circumstances that brought him by, near or through Bogota, Colombia.

Weak Spot: One factor, though, overrides all others. Occasionally John finds himself taking cases he knows he shouldn't when he's already overloaded and has bad vibes about the assignment. Why? Beneath that business exterior every detective is a human being with a highly individualized personality and a unique complex of experiences. John, for instance, has two sons and has seen more than his share of child neglect, child abuse and even child homicide cases. So for reasons he can't fully understand, when a client tells him that his ex has kidnapped their ten-year-old daughter and fled to Maine, John finds two of his organs immediately involved — his ears and his heart. Marilyn Greene has likewise expressed a kinship with people whose children are lost. John has recovered thirty-seven kidnapped children. He freely admits it's his most important work, for he has come to believe that noncustodial kidnapping is the most subtle form of child abuse.

Selling Yourself

This is the other side of the coin during the initial interview. While PIs are doing all the aforementioned assessment, they're also functioning as their own PR/sales force, and what they are selling is themselves. Small-town investigators don't worry as much about this angle as their big-city counterparts because there's rarely competition. On the other hand, they are concerned because the already nervous potential client may decide that hiring a PI isn't what is desired after all.

So the detective walks a fine line between being overbearing and barely competent. The detective tries to maintain a professional demeanor without being intimidating, abrasive or aloof. The detective also tries to show some personal concern, but not so much as to seem like prying. Objectivity is needed to assess a client's case, but too much makes the detective seem distant. So the detective is careful about actions and appearance. Food and drink costs are split. A suit is worn. Hands and face are clean. The detective is primarily a listener. Questions are asked only to elicit fuller responses. Eye contact and leaning forward are emphasized to show concern.

Summary

A current commercial uses the tagline "You don't get a second chance to make a first impression." This statement applies to both the detective and the client. How important is it that the detective weigh all the noted factors? John answers bluntly that his life depends upon it.

Hints

1. Just as the PI makes a great deal from the first meeting with the client, you as a writer should devote much energy to the first impression the client — almost always a major character — makes on the reader. Take into account the client's physical appearance (dress and grooming), mannerisms and body language. These client characteristics give you a lot of options. Does your PI note the rapid eye movement? Does your PI comment on the client's faux fur? Does your PI fail to realize the fake Rolex on the wrist?

2. Remember, the initiation of client relationships applies both to the PI and to you. Since most PI novels open with the detective meeting the client for the first time, you as a writer are not only writing this scene, but you're initiating relationships with your audience — and editor. This chapter is the most important in the book, but not necessarily the first chapter you write.

TAKING THE CASE

"So," Carolyn said, wiping the dew from her emerald eyes, *"where do we go from here?"*

"I hit the pavement," I said. *"You go home and get a good night's sleep."*

"But what about a retainer?"

"I trust you."

"How much is this going to cost me? What do you get a day?"

"Later."

"Expenses?"

"When I'm done, we'll settle up."

"A contract?"

I squeezed her hand. "That's all the contract I need."

Richard Steele,
Josh Shepherd, PI

In this scene at least Richard Steele brought up financial and legal matters. In too much PI fiction, we stress again, money and contracts are never even mentioned; at best, they're dealt with between chapters one and two. The PI comes across in these stories as a noble piece of work, an independently wealthy crusader who rights wrongs for the good of humanity and personal satisfaction. Conversely, two of John's most basic guidelines are "Don't die" and "Don't starve to death." The PI wants to make a profit, and the contract, rates, per diems and expenses are an integral part of that reality.

In this respect one of the most realistic detective writers we know is Sue Grafton. Throughout Grafton's alphabet series, Kinsey Millhone ponders some very practical concerns—how much should I charge? Can this client afford to pay? Can my fee keep my VW going one more day? In real life the fee and the negotiations for it are more important to the PI than the choice of weapons or vehicle; in fact, the fee and the collection of it may determine whether the PI drives a Buick or a Bug.

Contracts

As with so many other aspects of the trade, contracts vary in relation to the size of the agency and its location. Obviously, big-city operations have standard, multipage documents written in great detail. In fact, clients usually need attorneys to check over the specifics. Smaller agencies have smaller contracts. Some firms really do operate on a handshake basis. Small-town PIs often fall into this category. Ed Hino, who operates out of a small town, Lansdale, Pennsylvania, prefers not to deal in written contracts. Verbal acceptances and terms suffice.

Most contracts specify the exact nature of the assignment, the detective's daily rates, types and range of covered expenses, time frame, maximum amounts to be spent, penalty clauses, and even bonuses for such things as court dates and prompt delivery of the client's goal. Large agencies may have pre-existing contracts and be on retainer.

Operating by himself in a small town, John has evolved a somewhat unique form. He doesn't use a contract as such. He usually has his clients sign a paper acknowledging that "We the undersigned have empowered John Landreth to work for us in a matter of grave consequence." Without hamstringing John with all sorts of specific requirements, this form gives him minimal legal leverage, and if the police or others need proof he is indeed working for the party he claims, John simply has to present the document. Of course, there are many instances where he can't use such a document since his client's confidentiality is of paramount importance. (See sample contract next page.)

Rates

Because of the changing economy, all rates mentioned here are already outdated. Moreover, other factors cause variation in them. But, the following will give you a sense of how a PI's rates are determined and what the PI is paid.

- Location: Just as the cost of living in the Boston-New York-Hartford triangle is higher than that in Lexington, Kentucky, so the rates a PI from that area charges will be higher. And even in Lexington, the rates will be higher than in surrounding rural counties.

- Assignment: Another factor is the type of job the client wants. Firms specializing in computer fraud, for instance, must charge more to cover the cost of the high tech equipment plus the training required of its employees to operate that equipment.
- Legal Consequences: Cases that will necessitate court appearances and depositions cost more.
- Danger: Rates rise in direct proportion to the degree of difficulty, especially as the job can place the PI in jeopardy. A detective will charge less for simply having to make a phone call to a state agency than for trekking into the Mexican desert to rescue a child from a drug dealer.
- Local vs. Travel: In-town cases usually have lower rates than

---

John Landreth
Criminal and Missing Persons Investigations

709 West Main Street   (606)623-8449
Richmond, Kentucky

To Whom It May Concern

As of this date, August 29, 1981, I the undersigned have retained the services of John Landreth, Private Detective, to represent me as my lawful attorney in fact in a matter of deep personal importance to me. I hereby impower Mr. Landreth to act in and for me in my best interest. To this end I have tendered $2,000 to serve as an expense retainer in the above matter.

Further the affiant saith not.

_____

A sample contract used by John Landreth.

out-of-town cases. In fact, in the former, the PI probably charges by the hour; out of town, a flat fee/day.

- Experience: An inexperienced PI usually charges less than the seasoned veteran, but the veteran probably has a better chance of solving the problem faster.

- Payability: Sometimes the cost of a case comes down to the personality of the detective. John hasn't let it be known (until now), but since he operates in a poor area with so many families living near the poverty line, he often charges his clients what he knows they *can* pay. A richer client gets charged more.

- Economics 101: Sometimes it comes down to the law of supply and demand. In a large city with lots of agencies, a PI's rates must be competitive. On the other hand, small-town PIs without a great deal of competition can charge whatever the market will bear.

So what are real-life PIs across the country charging?

In Cincinnati, for instance, nonspecialty detectives usually charge $30 to $70 an hour for in-town cases. Out-of-town investigations run around $500/day and higher.

Outside of Philadelphia Ed Hino gets $50/hour plus expenses (.35/mile).

In San Francisco Josiah Thompson's hourly rate is about $100. That's twenty times what he made as a "green" (rookie) operator back in 1976.

In Miami Mike Ackerman of The Ackerman Group, though he specializes in hostage negotiation, offers divergent services. He operates Risknet, a twenty-four-hour-a-day service that he sends out to PC's through telephone lines. Companies such as Chevron and Mobil, which operate overseas, are willing to spend up to $8,500 per year to subscribe. Ackerman also trains bodyguards and assesses the kidnap-proof facilities at office sites and residences. For this service he may bill his clients a flat fee of $1,000/day.

In Los Angeles John Lynch gets more than $60/hour for his agents. For a simple background check he might charge a client a flat fee of around $200.

In Buffalo Robert Ferrari charges $500 a day plus expenses. With a million-dollar liability policy and a van carrying more than $100,000 worth of surveillance equipment, he has to cover his costs somehow.

In Washington, D.C. Robert Peloquin, President of Intertel, has more than sixty investigators. Each gets $125/hour plus expenses. Mongoven, Biscoe and Duchin, a firm in the same town, specializes in investigating social activists. For around $3,500/month it will look into the activities of one of these groups. Goldstein & Denton get more than $100/hour.

In London, England, by way of comparison, Lindy Grant charges $70/hour for a pair of her operatives to tail a suspected philandering husband.

In New York William Callahan of Unitel gets about $100/hour plus expenses. However, he has an army of informers, and if he pays one $1,000 for a desired piece of information, the client is billed that amount. Jules Kroll of Kroll Associates charges by the job, which is usually looking into mergers and acquisitions. A quick check of a company might net $100,000. For a lengthy takeover defense, Kroll once billed a client $6 million.

Upstate in Schenectady Marilyn Greene, who specializes in finding lost persons, charges her clients by the case. A couple in Louisville paid her $1,800 plus expenses in 1983 to help find their daughter, who still hasn't been located.

On an average, then, right now a competent PI gets about $100/hour plus expenses.

Expenses

"Plus expenses" is a fairly common phrase in the trade, but what does it mean? The truth is it means whatever the detective wants it to. Some expenses are explained and agreed to in advance; others just show up on the bill — and for a good reason. No detective can completely anticipate all the expenses that will be incurred during the course of an investigation.

Common expenses include travel (e.g., gas, plane fare), lodging and food. Along the way the detective occasionally has to pay informants as well as purchase one-time-only equipment (see chapter seventeen, "Making It Happen"). If the piece of equipment is a permanent addition to the arsenal and will see plenty of future duty, the PI probably won't charge the whole amount to the client.

Extraordinary expenses also occur. On more than one occasion John has had to procure the services of a prostitute. He has been known to hire local actors, sometimes taking them out of state for a job. Once, in a childnapping case, John even rented a conference room at a local motel, hired a phony photographer and had the whole affair catered.

Receipts are something a smart detective never fails to keep. Not only are they necessary to justify expenses on a client's bill, but the PI's accountant needs to have them. Still, when was the last time you read a book where the PI dropped a receipt for filling his gas tank into a brown envelope with the client's name on it, or even presented the client with a bill?

Billing

Within ten days after the close of a case, a PI presents an itemized bill with the final report (see sample bill, chapter eighteen). John likes to wrap up a case quickly, and since the client is usually quite grateful when the report is presented, that offers the PI a positive moment to hand over the bill and collect. Large firms might bill strictly by mail, but John likes his final contact to be personal. Large firms can have the machinery in place to take credit cards. John prefers hard cash, but will settle for checks on local banks. For out-of-town clients a cashier's check or cash is his preferred mode of payment.

As we said earlier, clients do stiff detectives. Since detectives are often in the collection business, this practice would seem risky, but clients do it all the time. Detectives, though, are experts at getting their money. By going to court? Any small business trying to collect an unpaid balance of under $1,000 knows that clients often gamble on the biller not having the time or energy to collect small sums. Even when small claims courts award judgments to the biller, that is still no guarantee of payment. Some PI's sole criterion for taking a case is the client's ability to pay just so this unpleasant situation never arises.

John's solution? He doesn't go to court. He doesn't even harass. But from the moment he starts a case he begins to learn something about the client. Along the way he makes other discoveries about his client's private life, and more often than not he finds something the client would prefer not made public. Welchers realize that if they don't pay, John can waive confidentiality. And, as John says, "Letting the cat out of the bag in a small town can produce an aroma that kitty litter can't hide."

Once John was stiffed by a client. When he went to cash a $2,500 check, he discovered the client had only $2,000 in the bank. In a fictional mystery, John had read about a detective depositing enough money in another person's account to cover the check, so he went to one window of the client's bank and put $500 in the client's account, making sure it was posted immediately. At another window he presented the client's check and withdrew the entire amount. So a $500 investment (plus the cost of a paperback mystery) was worth $2,000.

Some detectives take partial payment in advance. Ed Hino collects $400 (one day's pay at $50/hour) from the average citizen before starting on a case. If he needs another day's work on that case, he asks for that money beforehand. With attorneys and insurance companies, he sends bills, but acknowledges both are notoriously slow in paying.

Milking the Case

The scene is familiar on TV. The distraught client asks the detective how fast the missing loved one can be found. The PI stares into those grief-stricken eyes and answers, "As fast as I can." In real life, all PIs are not this scrupulous. Which is the basic problem with paying per diems. Think about it. If a PI has been mostly out of work lately, is it in his best financial interest to solve the case in haste?

As a result, some unethical PIs string along clients. They purposefully supply them with just enough information to keep the client interested, but not enough to provide a solution to the case. Such a crime pays and offers the PI little chance of being caught.

Rotten Apple—The Staller

This type of PI is first and foremost a con artist. While the cowboy (see page 54) often places people in physical jeopardy, the staller puts the client in financial jeopardy. Stallers are often big advertisers, luring clients with cheaper rates. They cast a lot of lines into the water; when they find a client willing to pay and with a protractable case, they strike.

Stallers love missing persons and divorce cases where their

clients' emotional involvement blinds them to the PI's activities. Stallers, like mine-salters (see page 42), feed the client just a little success, dangle some hope and hold out for more money. In the con artist's world, this technique is known as "the draw out."

Summary

Your treatment of such practical matters as contracts, rates, per diems and expenses depends greatly upon your PI's experience, the location and size of his/her operation, the nature of the case and the amount of travel involved. You must have a firm grasp on the often hard realities of the business world to make your detective as credible as possible.

Hints

1. As a writer, you've got to do a little more work than Richard Steele. When you choose a locale for your PI, you're best off talking to a real-life PI from that area about some of these specifics. Find out what the going rate is. Determine how specific the contract is. And keep in mind that since most PIs do their own PR, they may exaggerate.

2. Even more important, you've got to know your fictional PI well. After all, the local going rate doesn't matter if your PI is unscrupulous or independently wealthy. Once again we stress that you can't get under your detective's skin or write from the inside out until you grasp that a PI is primarily a businessperson.

3. In so much PI fiction today, the detective seems to work cases devoid of economics, at least as far as fees and expenses are concerned. Ironically, the first fictional detective, Poe's C. Auguste Dupin, was extremely concerned with money. In fact, he refused to divulge the hiding place of the purloined letter until the Prefect of Police, of all people, paid him 50,000 francs.

4. You might draw up a contract for your PI and run it by a lawyer friend to see if it omits or conflicts with any key point of law in your locale.

T W E L V E

SURVEILLANCE

I spotted Phil Landers, Carolyn's wandering-eye husband, as he strolled out of the Wallace Building, where he worked. Good old Phil wasn't alone. He was wearing his brassy-haired secretary like a cheap cologne. I took the elevator with them down to the parking garage. Then my flame-red Ferrari stuck to his BMW's rear end like a HONK IF YOU LOVE WHALES bumper sticker. I kept hanging out my window to let the camcorder catch the happy couple closerthanthis, hugging and kissing like teenagers in heat.

Richard Steele,
Josh Shepherd, PI

Ask PIs how they spend most of their time and the answer will probably be "legwork." A major part of a case is often surveillance, the clandestine observation of a person, place or thing. As with other parts of the business, the detective usually gets better with experience. Certain things work — others don't. The key is that there is a methodology to it, a process wherein proper preparation and correct procedure most often lead to success.

Purpose

Why surveil a place? One reason might be because the PI wants to be sure what's going on inside — e.g., gambling, cockfighting, illicit sex. The place might also be a known hangout of someone the PI wants to find, and if the PI can't find that person, a known acquaintance might do. While John's not too sure about ghosts haunting particular spots, he's a great believer in people being creatures of habit, that they constantly return to familiar haunts even when they know they shouldn't. Or as he puts it, "Study the mouse, not the maze." If John's looking for a jai alai lover he knows has fled from Florida to somewhere in Connecticut, he might stake out the Hartford Fronton. People who disappear give up their identities, not their habits.

Why surveil a person? Usually to gather information and evidence. The person under surveillance also might lead the PI to somebody more desired. Tailing a philandering husband might not only uncover a love nest, but a piece of property that the couple actually has in common, property that should be part of a divorce settlement. While the police might tail a suspect in the belief that a crime is about to be committed, John usually comes in after the crime—or during an ongoing affair.

Why surveil a thing? Some objects need to be protected. John has been hired to watch horses and cars, the latter because the client fears his once-vandalized vehicle is still a target. John has also staked out drops, public places where money has been left, to make certain that 1) nobody mistakenly picks it up and 2) he can follow who does pick it up.

Preparation

Successful surveillance begins with bringing along the proper equipment—shades, newspapers, the wide-mouthed bottle, a roll of quarters, some cash (singles are good so that the PI comes close to exact amounts with bills and taxis that must be hurriedly paid), a credit card, an ice pick, maps, camera, paper and pencil, binoculars and simple disguises (e.g., a baseball hat). To help him pass the time, John usually throws in a bad paperback mystery so that he doesn't get too engrossed (Richard Steele is a good bet). PIs working as a team usually establish procedure (e.g., "the drag" who assumes the tail position directly behind the subject and/or "the point" in front of the subject). If the subject is not known, a PI may study a picture, previous reports on the subject, or in some cases police reports. A PI also tries to ascertain the level of danger involved by asking questions: Is the subject prone to violence? Is the subject known to carry a weapon? Has the subject been arrested? If so, for what? How recently? Finally, detective teams, like their fictional counterparts Dick Tracy and Sam Ketchem, check out their communication equipment (probably not two-way wrist radios), especially their power source (usually batteries) and the frequency to which they are attuned.

Types of Surveillance

Stationary. PIs choose vantage points that allow them to keep careful tabs on a place, person or object. Sometimes these locales are a rented room, a borrowed vantage point, a rooftop or a parked car. Secrecy is a major goal, so binoculars, cameras with telephoto lens and possibly high tech listening devices are employed. The detective chooses appropriate clothing so as to blend in. Sunglasses and newspapers are minimal props to keep the suspect from "burning" the detective. John even has a pair of sunglasses with mirrors on the sides so that he can see behind him. While the device sounds like something the Three Stooges might wear, it is a highly effective way of surveying an area without letting a suspect look him directly in the face; John appears to be looking the opposite way. John has also been known to poke a hole in a newspaper or duct tape a small mirror to the inside of the paper. In a fixed position he tries to take notes on what he observes both for future reference and to keep himself alert.

Moving: Foot. Here the large firm has the advantage over the one-person op. In truth, following a subject alone is an almost impossible task for the PI, despite the frequency with which TV and movies use this technique. In wide-open spaces it's easy for a subject to spot a single tail. Also, if the subject walks a couple of blocks, then suddenly hops into a vehicle—public or private conveyance—there's little PIs, far removed from their vehicles, can do. Ever try to hail a taxi in a small town or Manhattan? Maintaining the proper distance while alone is difficult. Too close, you're burned; too far, you lose the subject or can't observe his/her actions with sufficient detail. Three tailers, on the other hand, can alternate the lead position, cover contingencies (such as keeping one person with a vehicle), work one behind and one beside, as well as the other tail positions.

Moving: Vehicle. As with on-foot tactics, there's a major difference between one-person and team surveillance. Again, the ideal is three or more cars. With the ABC method, often used by federal agents, A-car follows a block behind the subject, B-car stays a block behind A-car, and C-car runs parallel to the subject on another street. A second method involves only two cars; A and B constantly alternate in the block-behind position. Radio/phone communication among or between the vehicles is essential to coordinate these activities. One car is almost impossible. In the city, it's too easy to lose the subject due to traffic jams and lights; in the open, a detective can be burned faster than a fair-haired baby in the summer sun.

When John finds himself alone in such surveillance, he has to resort to his bag of tricks to beat the odds. Occasionally he hires another operative to act as his eyes and ears while he drives. Two, he marks the subject's car. In the daylight he prefers to spray paint the bumper with a bright color. More than once he has painted the top of a car and used a helicopter to follow it. At night he ice picks a small hole in the subject's taillight (being careful not to break the bulb), then sticks to that distinctive shaft of white light coming out the hole that makes the subject's car stand out from the herd of red lights.

Inside. An undercover operation is a specialized, complicated, dangerous and rare form of surveillance. The detective becomes a spy in the enemy camp. With a PI this covert work usually lasts a very short time. While the FBI and CIA can spend long hours and lots of money manufacturing a phony identity (as well as supporting it) and training an agent to go "in place," the PI doesn't usually have the experience, the time or the ability to role-play. Sure, John can pull on his cowboy boots and baseball cap to pass for a local in another city, and he knows enough of the jargon, accent, clipped speech and mannerisms to sustain the illusion for a couple of rounds. On the other hand, John will never be foolish enough to attempt to pass himself off as a computer consultant or a mathematics professor.

Obvious. Although by its very nature surveillance is supposed to be secret, a detective at times wants to stir the pot. If things aren't happening, and if detectives can't obtain what's needed any other way, they might try to make things happen. One way to pressure subjects is to make them very much aware they are being watched. Very often people under pressure do stupid things. To drive two lovers who are playing it cool into the daylight and each other's arms at nightfall, John might make a nuisance of himself with the weaker. John likes to panic people into making desperate phone calls. He once let himself be seen so that the suspect, who had a cellular

Surveillance can be done either on foot (top photo) or in a vehicle (bottom photo).

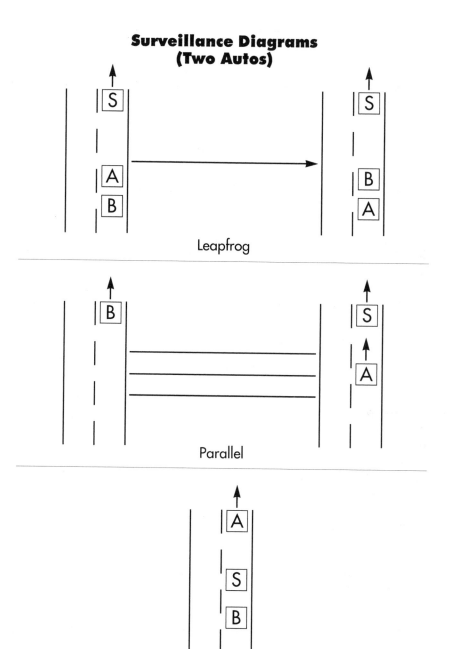

Surveillance Diagrams
(Two Autos)

Leapfrog

Parallel

Leading

phone, would call her partner. John knew the phone's frequency and listened in on the whole thing.

Bugged By Phones?

Every time the President makes a phone call from Air Force One it's not necessarily private. Technocreeps can eavesdrop. Fortunately, the government scrambles such calls. Unfortunately, people using cellular and cordless phones rarely realize the potential for lost privacy or have the technology for scrambling.

Is listening in on broadcast calls legal? In 1986 Congress outlawed eavesdropping on cellular phone calls, but not cordless telephones, headsets or FM walkie-talkies. Federal legislation is pending to prohibit the manufacture of scanners able to receive cellular frequencies.

So, right now you need to watch those phone calls and remember that an enterprising PI could easily intercept both your cellular and cordless conversations.

Summary

To make your PI believable, you should be aware of proper methodology for surveillance. This process involves knowing the valid purposes of surveillance of a location, person or object; the proper equipment needed; and the various types of surveillance possible (including the advantages and difficulties of each).

Hints

Successful PIs develop a list of do's and don'ts. To a degree you can control your audience's response by whether or not your PI adheres to the following guidelines.

1. Don't have your PI drink on the job. As mentioned earlier, alcohol retards the PI's reactions, distorts perceptions and forces frequent trips to the john (where the subject probably isn't). Sure, if the subject enters a bar, the detective may need a drink to blend in, as Ed Hino says, "Like gin with vermouth," but drinking should not be a habitual action. Even drinking

coffee and Cokes during a stakeout are a no-no. Because they contain so much caffeine, both are diuretics.

2. Before starting a surveillance, establish a priority point between gaining information and getting burned. Many detectives will claim that the most important goal in surveillance is not being seen. John thinks the whole practice is a question of risk. How important is the information the surveillance is seeking? When does the possibility of getting burned justify the risk of trying to obtain information? The answer usually involves time constraints, the severity of the assignment and the client's ability to pay.

3. A PI can learn from the movies. Just because this book has looked down on most TV and cinematic sleuths doesn't mean that some of their tricks don't work. Because he surveils a lot, John reads a lot and occasionally runs across ploys worth trying. For instance, he thinks that whoever did the research for Polanski's *Chinatown* deserves a gold medal. Just like J.J. Gittes, John stuck a watch under a parked car so that he could determine what time the car moved. He's found that tiger-striping the watch in tape holds it together (and digital watches won't work). From still another fictional private eye, John learned an interesting variation on the ice pick-in-the-taillight trick. When he couldn't get close enough to the subject's car to pick it, John punctured the red plastic lens with a BB gun.

4. Women detectives have a difficult problem answering nature's call while surveilling (even the wide-mouth bottle may not be sufficient).

5. Surveillance by car is extremely tough. Clients always think it will be a piece of cake. Also, communication is difficult.

6. Have your detective double-check that equipment. John knew a PI who was asphyxiated because he left his motor running during surveillance and the side window to his station wagon down slightly. The culprit was a faulty muffler.

7. Be aware of current technology. A cassette player in working condition gives a slight diversion to the PI while allowing for time to listen to previous surveillance tapes (don't forget to check for fresh batteries). A firm in Miami makes a combination binocular-camera. Another firm sells a starlight scope.

They could be in your PI's trunk because even if they're too expensive to purchase, they could be leased.

8. A single car can be made to look like two different vehicles in the dark simply by using the headlights one time, fog lights the next.

9. A surveilling detective must be inconspicuous. Dark cars, drab clothes and no flashy bankrolls are the order of the day. Walking a dog or running in a jogging suit gets the detective into most neighborhoods without looking suspicious. The big outfits like "Pinks" and Burns, who use a lot of ex-cops and pensioned-off police, are notorious for having two men in suits and ties sit in residential neighborhoods reading newspapers and drinking coffee at 10:30 in the morning. Do you think their "plain wrapper" (unmarked car) stands out? Of course they can justly charge the client for so many hours of surveillance, but this time the game knows that something is afoot, Watson.

10. A good detective never locks eyes with a person under surveillance. People remember people they get a good look at. A detective doesn't point the surveillance car at the subject but rather uses the rearview mirror.

11. A small-town detective might get away with running into a subject under surveillance a couple of times. But in the big city nobody buys such a coincidence. Of course, in a big city nobody pays much attention to anybody else either.

12. A detective is patient. A detective is patient. A detective is patient. John likes to quote Charlie Chan: "Softly, softly catchee monkey." John also remembers the brochure of a large PI firm in L.A. that after pointing out what they did, emphasized, "We do nothing quickly."

13. Even the best detectives lose more subjects than they successfully surveil.

14. Use your imagination. John even learned something from Homer. Once during the holiday season, John had himself delivered to a subject's house wrapped up as a large Christmas present. Inside the unopened box, he observed and videotaped the subject engaged in several ambulatory activities atypical of a person confined to a wheelchair. The necessary information secured, John "unwrapped" himself and walked out of the

house to the subject's gape-jawed amazement.

15. Keep Landreth's Law in mind. Murphy's Law states that if something can go wrong, it will. Landreth's is a more pessimistic corollary: Everything you planned will go wrong, things you haven't planned will foul you up, and Mother Nature and geography will conspire against you. If you have to be out in the sun, it will be too hot. If you must remain outside, it will be winter. It will rain/sleet/snow at the exact moment you need to take that picture through a telephoto lens. Those blinds you broke in a subject's room yesterday so you could peer through them today have been repaired. The nearest pay phone is always out of order. Automatic toll booths will malfunction. Your engine will flood, you will have vaporlock and diarrhea, or your lights will be left on, yielding a dead battery. Yesterday's two-way street will be one-way when you get there in a hurry. That driveway you picked out yesterday to watch your subject from will be filled with cars today.

Things will happen to the other guy, too, that foul up the detective's best-laid plans. He will have car trouble or wreck right in front of you and ask you to be a witness for his insurance claim. Once in Phoenix, Arizona, John was following a 240 Datsun in a chartered Bell helicopter. The object was to tail the subject to his house to recover a child kidnapped by the noncustodial parent. After thirty-three miles a female cop pulled the guy over just as he hit the Scottsdale city limit. The male chauvinist in him must have come out, for instead of ticketing the guy, she arrested him, took him to jail and had his 240Z towed in. All the while John circled helplessly overhead at 750 feet. Three days of work and 800 miles of surveillance came close to being blown.

But another of John's laws says that if you are given lemons, make lemonade. From the air he tailed the tow truck to the police impound, then got the subject's new address from the arrest blotter (at the jail the subject had given his real address, hoping to be released on his own recognizance). By the time the subject got out and went home, John and the mother, who had legal custody, had been there and recovered the child from the housekeeper.

T H I R T E E N

LOCATING RECORDS

In Macon I had a lot of time to kill outside the Whoopy Motel. Whoever said that "Nothing's as boring as someone else's love life — unless they're unclothed" was a genius. Macon Whoopy Motel rooms didn't have windows, but they did have cheap sheets and hourly rates. So, while I waited, I used my cellular phone to call my friend Emmy Lou at the DMV. In five minutes I had a list of all five cars Phil Landers owned. If I ever got out of this business, boy did I have a future in research!
Richard Steele,
Josh Shepherd, PI

After the agrarian age and the industrial revolution, we Americans are now entering the era of information, a period historians claim will be dominated by the computer. As a result, there is a great deal of information out there about almost everybody. The trick is knowing how and where to obtain it. Unfortunately, such knowledge usually takes a bit more than the TV-PI fiction cliché of a little phone call to a friend. In real life, detectives try to cultivate low friends in high strategic places. But all detectives won't use such tactics. Ed Hino refuses to ask former FBI colleagues to tap sources of information because he knows if they did, it would jeopardize their careers.

The boom in technology has given birth to one of the newest clichés in the mystery genre. Instead of old-fashioned legwork and long, patient research, the PI simply visits an old friend, the computer hacker. Whenever Magnum needed information, he simply called Mac at Naval Intelligence, whose knowledge was limited to every fact known to modern technology. On *Wiseguy*, supernerd Vinnie dialed his "Uncle," who seemed to have access to Mac's Omni-science 2000 computer.

The truth is that the detective, along with the rest of us, has entered the computer age and can access a wealth of data. However, much research involves legwork, cultivating friends in the right places (networking) and simply knowing where to go.

Let's put your detective in Josh Shepherd's gumshoes. If you really wanted your PI to discover a great deal of information about one Phil Landers, where would you send him/her and what could be found?

Essentially, there are three major sources of information: local, state and federal. In addition, countless other records exist in the private sector, which, surprisingly, can be harder to access without official sanction than some state and local government ones.

Here are some excellent sources and the data that can be found with each agency.

Local

Board of Education: Subject's record as student/employee, including grades, attendance, extracurricular activities, disciplinary action, honors. Recent records also contain test results, personality profiles, IEP's (Individualized Education Plan in Special Ed). If the records have been sent somewhere else, the original will contain the forwarding address (which is useful in locating children or parents who change locations). Don't forget college records from registrars, placement offices, alumni associations, fraternities and sororities; old annuals, often found in the school library or alumni house, usually contain dated but useful photos. These provide legal ways of circumventing the Buckley Amendment about student privacy rights.

Family Education and Privacy Act (Public Law 93-380)

This 1974 federal law deals with colleges' and universities' maintenance, inspection and release of student records. The law spells out the rights and restrictions on these records—who has access to them and who doesn't. These records include such things as transcripts, test scores, evaluations, correspondence, admission forms and biographical data. At most schools, advisors, academic deans and the named student have open access to them. Students, though, are barred from confidential letters inserted into their records before January 1, 1975, school medical and police records, and their parent's confidential financial statements. The law also mandates that students be notified when their files are accessed and gives them the right to challenge, in hearings if necessary, the content of these documents.

What outsiders may view these records? The list includes parents, the Comptroller General of the United States, the Secretary of HEW and the head of other relevant federal programs that support schools. Records can also be procured with a subpoena or other judicial order. Other persons desirous of these documents must go through the individual student, who must provide a release. This release must:

- be written
- specify which records are wanted
- note the reason for the release.

Obviously, then, these records are difficult for a PI to touch — legally.

Voting Registry: Subject's name, address, Social Security number, place of birth, occupation, signature, length of residency and former residencies are all possibilities.

Licensing: To determine whether the subject is operating a legally registered business. Lists usual information. Contains D/B/A's (Doing Business As).

City Clerk: Subject's birth certificate (may include date, place, mother's maiden name, father, attending physician); death certificate (may include parents' names, next of kin, cause of death, funeral director, cemetery); marriage certificate; licenses for cars, boats and other vehicles; plat books for property (exact location, owner, restrictions); deeds, mortgages, liens and other legal documents.

Tax Assessor: Subject's intangible and real property (with location, purchase price, current assessed value).

County Farm Bureau: Atlases and plat books. Owners of rural property.

Court (Superior, County, District): Civil, criminal, juvenile and probate. Suits, divorces and criminal actions. Information on awards, sentences, appeals, contracts, bankruptcy and personal injury. Many also keep traffic tickets on microfilm, which provides a way of determining a subject's height, weight, hair and eye colors and Social Security number.

Public Library: Check phone books, local newspaper copies, historical records (check local historical societies too), and to see if the subject has a library card. City codes, up-to-date state statutes, specialized directories (civic, business, lawyers, doctors) in large cities. *Cole's Directory*, available in metropolitan areas only, lists for each city 1) street addresses, 2) phone numbers, 3) names; arranged all three ways so that if you know any one entry, you can find the other two.

Others: Judge-Executive (county leaders), Coroner, Sheriff, Fire Marshall, Health Department, Civil Codes (building restrictions), Police, ex-teachers:

- Better Business Bureau
- Local credit bureau
- Chamber of Commerce/Tourism Bureau
- Community Development
- City/District/County Attorney
- Phone book
- Newspaper: copies

State

Department of Motor Vehicles (DMV): Drivers licenses, vehicle registration, plate numbers, ownership, license limitation, accidents, violations.

State Supreme Courts: Judgments for/against individuals, businesses.

ABC Authority: Control of liquor licenses.

Welfare Agencies: Various forms of public assistance.

Vocational Rehabilitation: Medical records of employees.

State Police/Highway Patrol: Investigations into state and local personnel. Records of motor vehicles, boats, criminal charges, firearms.

Health Authority: Registry of doctors, malpractice investigations.

Attorney-General: Investigation of city, county and state problems.

State Library: State statutes, city codes.

Bureau of Prisons: Records of inmates, charges.

Parole Board.

Others: Fish and Game, Fire Marshall, Consumer Affairs, Business.

You Could Look It Up

Suppose your PI wants to know about a recent federal court decision? How about some state statute or securities law? They might tap into Westlaw, a computer-assisted legal research service. After the initial hookup, the user is charged by the time on-line.

And all without letting your fingers wander from the keyboard.

Federal

Social Security: Employment records. Access only to individual, parent or relative.

Immigration and Naturalization Service (INS): Registry of all aliens.

Post Office.

Securities and Exchange Commission (SEC): Records of all public companies, stockbrokers, investment services. SEC Litigation Index, Broker-Dealer File (financial statements), Investment Adviser File.

Federal Court: Supreme, District.

Law & Order: FBI, CIA, DEA, Justice Department.

Veterans Administration (V.A.).

Department of Transportation.

Treasury: Bureau of Customs, IRS, Secret Service.

Labor.

Department of Health and Human Services.

National Crime Information Center (NCIC): Records of stolen vehicles, articles, firearms, securities, wanted/missing persons, fingerprints.

Using the IRS as Your Investigator

The IRS isn't all bad. In fact, one positive is the use of their huge database to locate someone who needs to be told of a serious illness, inheritance, or of a lost relative seeking them. Of course, Wiley Detective could probably think of a way to . . .

General: Private Sector

National newspapers: *Wall Street Journal, USA Today, New York Times.*

Telephone companies: National (AT&T, Sprint), regional (baby Bells), locals; reverse directories (crisscross information).

Insurance companies.

Associations: Almost every industry has its own association (medical = American Medical Association, attorneys = American Bar Association, professors = American Association of University Professors). Consult *Gale's Encyclopedia of Associations.*

Credit services: Almost every industry has its own credit organization with names of individual people plus businesses.

Labor unions.

National credit bureaus: TRW, Trans Union and Equifax dominate the consumer-data industry. The Big Three purchase records from banks and retailers monthly that detail the financial activities of almost every American consumer. Each company has approximately 150 million individual files.

National Automobile Theft Bureau (NATB): It maintains a data-bank of 2.5 million records and employs full-time agents to assist law enforcers in combating automobile crime. It also has 350 million manufacturers' records of assembly and shipping as well as Vehicle Identification Numbers (VINs).

Accessing the Information

Computers and contacts are often a shortcut to obtaining desired information. Unfortunately, learning how to use computers, finding a competent computer operator and establishing key contacts takes a great deal of time, effort and money. The dull truth is that to obtain the needed data the PI most often has to go workerlike through the normal pedestrian channels.

Finding some information is a piece of cake. At a public library, for instance, all your PI needs is a card and a helpful librarian. The best place to send your PI would be a college library, where s/he could consult various specialists (e.g., law librarian) or use computerized indexes. InfoTract and the Magazine Index allow the user to find sources on almost any topic, and the attached printer will provide you with a quick bibliography of the items you wish to investigate further.

Federal government offices are at the opposite end of the accessibility spectrum. Even if you know where your needle is located in the federal haystack, you may not be able to obtain it. So much of the information at the CIA, Department of State (e.g., passports) and Department of the Treasury is secret and confidential. The Federal Government is the nation's largest data bank. It was estimated in 1982, for instance, that the feds possessed more than 3.5 billion files — that works out to about fifteen per person. Under the Freedom of Information Act (1975) much of this data has been declassified and is available to consumers.

The Freedom of Information Act

The Freedom of Information Act (FOIA), enacted in 1966 and amended in 1974, makes it possible for the average citizen (including your PI) to obtain information contained in the files of federal agencies (all fifty states have passed similar open-records laws). A major purpose of the law is that individuals shouldn't have to demonstrate a reason for desiring the information; the burden of proof rests with the agency in question.

Government agencies, however, may legally withhold documents for any of nine reasons (i.e., "exemptions"):

- executive orders in the interest of national security
- information related to an agency's internal personnel policies
- statutory exemptions
- trade and financial information that is deemed privileged/confidential
- inter- and intra-agency materials not available to private parties engaged in litigation with those agencies
- invasions of personal privacy through personnel/medical files
- investigatory files completed for law enforcement purposes
- reports on financial institutions
- geological/geophysical data concerning wells

To discover which federal agency has the records you/your PI desires, you can consult the *U.S. Government Manual* (Government Printing Office, Superintendent of Documents, Washington, D.C. 20402, #D22-003-004245-8).

If you/your PI makes such a request, here are twelve tips to consider:

- be willing to pay all expenses (you can ask for charges in advance; asking for a waiver of fees is courting disaster and inviting delay)
- state your request in writing, not just a phone call
- note that your request is made "under the provisions of the Freedom of Information Act, 5 U.S.C. 552"
- comply with specific agencies' regulations; review the agency's policies and procedures before the request
- address the request to the proper agency; to be safe, put "FOIA REQUEST" on your envelope
- date your request (to set the compliance limit in motion and for your records)
- describe the desired materials accurately so that an agency employee can locate them with reasonable time and effort

- remind the agency of the ten-day compliance limit
- avoid categorical/general requests; be as specific as possible
- avoid exempt categories (the aforementioned nine)
- avoid information to be used in suits; the Department of Justice, in fact, requires that if litigation is your goal, you must so disclose with your initial request
- to expedite your request: keep a record of everything you do, don't violate agency policies, call the agency before and after your request, use certified and return-receipt requested mail (they get the request, you know the countdown date and you have a public record), and pressure the agency by phone if the ten-day limit is exceeded.

If you desire to check out a government office, you first need to get hold of the *Federal Government Registry*, which lists all federal departments, divisions and their leaders. Contact the department by phone or mail and ask for a release form. Fill it out and you may obtain what you want. They supposedly have ten days to respond. Obviously, the entire process takes time, and there's no guarantee you can get what you want. Note, too, that some offices, such as Social Security, will respond only to individuals, parents and relatives. Most of the time the key to entry is the subject's Social Security number. If you are stonewalled, you may refile. The agency in question then has twenty days to respond. While security, invasion of privacy and personnel memos are legitimate reasons for the agency to refuse your request, you then have the right to sue in federal court for the information.

On a state or local level, you can have your PI start the search with a phone book. Capital and individual cities will have a listing for all official departments, usually under City of _____ or State. Most states have a law enforcement telephone book that lists the various agencies county by county.

Of course you can shortcut the process by knowing about other national companies or hiring individual research firms. National Demographics & Lifestyles, for instance, is a virtually unknown data seller. Every time a consumer fills out a product warranty card, ND&L makes a permanent record of it. If your detective were chasing somebody who just had to have a new compact disc player, a call to ND&L would give you that buyer's last known address. If your PI had a personal computer, s/he could access Atlanta-based Information America. For $25 to $95 a month plus search charges, your detective need only type in the subject's name. The chances are better than one in three that IA knows that person's address, phone number, length of residence, court appearances, business dealings and property ownership. In the very near future, the best detective may well be the cleverest computer operator.

Your detective can probably get hold of a subject's credit history fairly easily. Such reports will list the subject's name, address, Social Security number, payment history, bankruptcies, liens, businesses that have requested the file, personal information (e.g., spouse, relatives) and comments the subject has added. Contrary to PI fiction myths, credit bureaus will not report how much money the subject has in banks, investments, criminal arrests, traffic tickets, purchased goods or medical history (however, this information can be obtained elsewhere). If you would like to be even more precise, you can write The Associated Credit Bureaus, Inc. (1090 Vermont Avenue NW, Suite 200, Washington, D.C. 20005-4905) to ask for a copy of a pamphlet on Consumers, Credit Bureaus and The Fair Credit Reporting Act.

Be aware that all credit bureaus will assure you that their data is available only to authorized, qualified people (Translation: anyone who will pay for it). John even knows some real PIs who break this rule and check into people's personal information purely as a pastime.

Releases

When Spenser needs vital information for a case, Robert Parker often has him break into a business to obtain it. Actually, there is a legal way to obtain confidential reports in the private sector. Your PI can use a release form. Suppose your detective needs some information about a client, witness or spouse's family. S/he first gets this person's permission in writing. A proper release form consists of the following:

- the PI's name (as being authorized to receive the desired information):
- specific record desired

- date
- subject's name
- subject's signature
- witness' name, signature and date
- any necessary information/restrictions (e.g., does the desired information relate to a specific accident?). These are usually obtained by attorneys who hire the detective.

Summary

You should be aware of the enormous amount of information on people and organizations available to your PI both in the private sector and through government agencies on the local, state and federal levels. Knowing which agencies to tap and the proper methodology for tapping them will give your fiction that air of verisimilitude.

Hints

1. Access varies from city to city, county to county, state to state.
2. The names of agencies also vary. Consult a phone book in that area for the specific title.
3. Obtaining federal data necessitates the filing of a form and a long wait.
4. Be patient.
5. If the material you need is for a court appearance, you will have to procure a certified copy for it to be admissible.
6. Very often the most vital information a PI discovers is the client's Social Security number. Note how prevalent this number is on client data. Very often you can obtain the Social Security number through records like a license or health insurance card and an automobile plate number.
7. It is best to call ahead to state and local authorities to discover what the regulations are pertaining to the desired information. You can also find out who is in charge.
8. Landreth's Law II: The higher you climb on the local-to-federal ladder, the harder it will be to obtain information.

9. Landreth's Law III: Money talks and po' folks walks. A "thanks for your help" lunch is not a bribe. A $20 bill for "copying costs" could be construed as overtipping.

10. You will have a great deal of trouble getting information from colleges and universities. The federal Department of Education has been advising institutions of higher learning recently that releasing information violates the Buckley Amendment. (See page 97.) John reminds us, however, that one school will usually divulge anything to another school over the phone if it's asked for in the proper jargon ("Hi, this is Aaron Holliday. I'm the Guidance Director at the Forrest School that Jarrod Banks is now attending. It would sure help us if you could give me some data off his last IEP.").

11. Don't totally forget the cliché of personal contacts obtaining desired information. Often a man can get data easier from a woman (and vice versa) than through same-sex channels. Civility, cordiality and flattery will open more doors than LAWS rockets or passkeys. John thinks that one of his main attributes is his ability to get help from overworked, underappreciated clerks.

12. A contemporary PI must be cognizant of the value of the computer, the existence of many data banks and the potential methods of interfacing with them. Most libraries, especially college, can supply you with the names of specific data services, their specialties, and especially those most apt to have what you want.

13. Most telephone information (caller, caller's number, caller's location, number dialed, number's location) takes a court order to obtain. On a local basis, a PI might be able to go to the nearest phone company and scan their files for a local resident's address, but it would probably cost something, and it would be up to the local company. John has heard of some hardball PI types who steal the phone bill from a subject's mailbox to see who has been called from that number; of course, John would never stoop to this tactic.

14. Access to bank files falls into a gray area. The best-case scenario is for your PI to have a friend in the bank. Otherwise a release/subpoena is necessary. Friends work in small towns. In big cities the strategy differs. The odds are that the bank clerk

won't know the account customer by sight, so if an enterprising PI knew the account number of the subject and only wanted a mini-statement or the copy of a few checks . . .

15. All the aforementioned sources are vulnerable to a good ruse or line of bull. The major exception is insurance companies, who only talk to other insurance companies. If a PI wished to try to talk his/her way into some closed information, John suggests the best time to call would be 12:01 P.M. All the management types are at lunch, leaving the more approachable to deal with callers. In fact, John has read mysteries where the detective has tried this, and assures us it still works.

16. Much information is freely obtained just by asking. To find the owner of a license plate, PIs don't need to file a form with the state Department of Motor Vehicles or cajole a friendly cop into tapping into the DMV computer. To obtain the name of a Kentucky vehicle owner, all we did was walk into the county clerk's office and give the plate number to one of five secretaries sitting there. No questions and ten seconds later we had the information. Had we known just the name of the owner or the car's VIN (Vehicle Identification Number), we could have found other information; any one piece leads to the others. License numbers are a matter of public record (as is much of the information in this chapter).

17. In twenty-six states and Washington, D.C., doctors and insurance companies have a better chance of viewing your medical records than you do. A PI working for an insurance company has about a fifty-fifty chance of getting these records easily. To find out what your state allows, you could ask a local doctor. If the PI works for a private citizen in a state where those records are denied, certain steps to obtain the records can be followed. In either case the easiest way for you to learn your state's rights as well as the whole process of accessing these records is to send ten dollars to Public Citizen, Department MRP, 2000 P. Street, Northwest, Washington, D.C. 20036 and ask for *Medical Records: Getting Yours.*

F O U R T E E N
THE INTERVIEW

As soon as good old Phil and Blondie checked out of their room, I checked out the motel clerk. He was a sixty-five-year-old man with a cane, a Santa Claus beard and a copy of Penthouse *under the motel register. At first he had memory lock about that nice couple that inhabited B2 on Tuesday nights. Fifty dollars and fifteen minutes later I had a chain of evidence that was going to tie Phil to a healthy settlement for his wife.*

Richard Steele,
Josh Shepherd, PI

Shepherd got his information by offering a positive incentive, money. The contrasting cliché in PI fiction occurs when the detective supplies the subject with a negative incentive—threatening to do physical/mental harm. In real life, PIs do spend much of their time interviewing a subject here, a suspect there, the subject's best friend, an eyewitness, an informant or a professional expert, but usually they don't have to resort to either of the hackneyed extremes. In fact, most detectives will admit that the major skill needed in their profession is being an expert interviewer; the best PI is often the best interviewer. As a result, some PIs are such specialists that they do nothing but interrogate.

Good interviewers have good technique. No matter how unprepared or spontaneous they seem, they actually have an agenda of what they wish to find out from each interviewee. They quickly figure out, whether through experience or instinct, the interviewee's personality and how to obtain the key information. Of course, occasionally PIs just happen to run into somebody connected with the investigation, and, if they're sharp, they can use these moments to make a case.

A case in point. John broke open a wrongful death investigation (which will be detailed later) after it had been "cold" for many months because he returned to an accident scene and bumped into an old man collecting recyclable cans. John is a great believer in luck being preparation meeting opportunity, so he struck up a conversation with the man about the famous accident in the very spot. The can-collector turned out to have arrived on the accident shortly after it happened and mentioned to John about a key witness taking hitherto unknown photographs of the wreck. To this day John believes that he wasn't lucky. He is willing to keep asking questions until he asks the right one; thus, he figures he would have eventually discovered the old man or someone else who knew of the photos.

Actually, there are as many different techniques and combinations thereof as there are PIs. However, most interviews have the same purpose and involve the same basic process—preparation, the interview itself and the follow-up.

Purpose

We live in an opinionated society in which almost everyone expresses views on the weather, politics, old movies and the Atlanta Braves' chances in the West. But detectives are not really interested in opinions (except by experts). What they want from the people they interview are concrete, very specific details—facts, observations (what they saw) or overhearings (what they heard, what they heard someone else say they heard). Not "What do you think about Gladys Kravitz next door?" but "What did you see and hear Gladys do on the night of June fifth at approximately 8:30?" An interview is conducted so that the detective can learn all the relevant facts the interviewee knows about the matter at hand. Even learning the interviewee knows nothing is learning something. Ultimately, though, a good detective not only learns the facts, but forms an opinion on the interviewee's credibility, personality, character, willingness to testify and the type of witness the interviewee might be in court.

Sometimes, though, the purpose is not pure fact-finding. Occasionally the interview is conducted as a catalyst. During the course of the interview, the detective deliberately divulges a particular piece of information that is calculated to cause the subject to react later. John has found, for instance, that when he gets involved with an A-B-C love triangle, he can lie to B about something A told him, knowing that the second he leaves B will try to get in touch with A.

Disinformation is a third purpose. The PI during the interview purposefully reveals a piece of untrue information, usually to a suspect. Occasionally, when he's working for an attorney, a PI might let some information "slip out" to the other side. The PI hopes this will lead the suspect/other side to base their future actions on that untruth.

Another noninformational purpose is the matter-of-fact interview, a question-and-answer show put on simply because it's expected. If John is investigating an out-of-town case, he might start by checking in with the local gendarmes to find out what they know. This is professional courtesy, like talking to the client's great aunt who likes company but rarely recalls her own name. John finds the real problem with these interviews is not the loss of time but that everyone has an opinion; he has to be careful not to let such opinions taint his objective view of the case.

Sometimes a PI might want to predispose a subject to a particular point of view. Can a person's recollections be slanted merely by how the PI asks a question or what questions are asked? John remembers asking one eyewitness to an assault if the sound of X hitting Y in the face was "like a two-by-four crushing a mush melon." The eyewitness simply nodded in the affirmative. Later, at the ensuing trial when the attorney for whom John worked asked the witness to describe the sound of X hitting Y, the witness testified it was "like a two-by-four crushing a mush melon."

Finally, John points out that based on what information he discovers during the interview, its purpose could change in midstream.

Preparation

In *Second Chance* Jonathan Valin has Cincinnati-based PI Harry Stoner proceed from person to person asking questions, then returning to ask more. That's realistic. However, almost never does Stoner think about what he's going to ask ahead of time. Rarely does he study previous notes or reports before the interview. As a result, until the denouement, Stoner misses the key information that, conveniently, is sitting in a file folder just waiting for him to read.

Knowledge is power. PIs like to have some idea of what they are getting into. For that reason, before the interview they try to obtain and review some of the records mentioned in the previous chapter. This data gives them a jumping-off point ("According to the accident report, you came along just minutes after . . ."). The data also supplies checks and balances.

One of John's rules is that he can't check out the tale until he's assessed the teller. Accordingly, John will pre-load information that allows him to cross-check the subject; in the interview he then asks questions to which he already knows the answers ("Oh, you were married before. Who to? I might know them . . . I see . . . Did you used to live up on Summit next to them?").

PIs also pre-check their equipment from the ubiquitous notepad and pen to the batteries in their tape recorder. John is a great believer in accurate records; therefore, he uses a recorder at most interviews. However, since he learned long ago that the presence of a recorder often intimidates and silences a subject, he went to a ruse. On his waist is what looks like a beeper; actually it will record for up to ninety minutes, and he has a permanent, reliable record without intimidation (at least more permanent and accurate than his memory).

Another piece of equipment that needs checking is the PI's appearance. As mentioned earlier, no matter the locale or social class of the subject, John wears a suit and is clean-shaven (portable razors are handy) to appear professional.

Probably the most important part of preparation is setting up the interview. While some interviews occur spontaneously, the PI prefers to make contact with the subject beforehand. Foremost in John's mind for most subjects is comfort. John finds that by allowing subjects to pick the time and place for an interview (though he might make suggestions), most people enter their comfort zone. Most people prefer to stay at their own home or business, so the PI usually goes to them.

Of course, there are some subjects John does not like to put at ease. If he knows/suspects/intuits they are nervous, he may try to intimidate them by suddenly confronting them or setting up some ruse to drive them to a spot they don't want to be.

The Interview Itself

Like the whole interview process, the interview itself can be broken down into several steps. While every investigator will not follow each step in all interviews, the steps suggest successful interviewing is usually a patterned procedure. The key to a good interview, though, is not technique alone, but control; ultimately the PI must dictate the path the conversation takes.

Rapport. Robert Frost once noted how difficult it is to hate somebody up close. The PI must get past hatred and/or indifference to establish a genuine relationship with the subject. First, the detective must come across as polite, friendly, conversational, interested and spontaneous. While the Joe Friday technique of "Just the facts" made good television, in real life, the interviewer gets more work out of a mule with a carrot than a stick. John finds that making small talk is a good way to begin. Sometimes he knows a subject's interests from records, sometimes experience and intuition tell him what to do, and often he simply "reads" the situation. For instance, if the subject makes ginseng tea, wears a Cincinnati Reds T-shirt or has a coffee table littered with *Cycle World* and *Motorcross Action Magazine*, John has three things to start with. But, John cautions, he can't let the small talk last too long or time and tiredness can detract from meaningful conversation. Also, John finds that subjects get interested in his profession. A good interviewer keeps in mind which one is the interviewee and which one is the interviewer.

Priming the Pump. Landreth's Law of Motion is that nothing halts a conversation as quickly as a "Yes" or "No" answer, and the ensuing silence wrecks whatever rapport has been established. For instance, the detective might start the actual interview segment with a question such as, "How did you happen to be at the scene of the accident?" The question offers both an easy way to open up the interviewee and a method to insure no "Yes" or "No" response. The PI also usually begins with questions of simple fact. Remember, your detective is not Alex Trebek testing the mental acumen of *Jeopardy* contestants. Your detective wants the interviewee to feel at ease, to believe s/he is an expert at what happened, and think s/he is a person with important information. In most cases such questions will have answers the detective already knows and can thus verify the interviewee's reliability, perception and willingness to cooperate. One question should lead to the next in logical sequence so that no one question appears more important than any other.

Interviewee Assessment. Step three begins in steps one and two. The experienced PI learns to "read" a subject—to figure out his/her personality type and what kind of approach works best. The FBI and other organizations on the cutting edge of interview theory currently use this highly structured and complex technique, which they call the kinesic (body language) method. However, this interview format is copyrighted and hence cannot be reproduced here or elsewhere.

In fact, John took a week off during the writing of this book to attend a course in its fundamentals. In assessment, the interviewer must decide: Is the subject self-centered or other-directed? Reticent or effusive? Needs prodding or likes to be left alone? Stimulated more by praise than criticism? John thinks the key to personality analysis is discovering what he calls the interviewee's "prime mover"—i.e., what force primarily motivates the subject? With men, John finds the answer is most often sex, money and/or power. Women, on the other hand, will usually be more responsive if they perceive the detective as a caring individual. John has had males admit to child-molesting and murder just by his pushing their power button. By showing a little understanding of women's domestic plights, he has gotten confessions to embezzlement, adultery and murder. John, then, sees the detective's role as dual. On one hand he's a chameleon, constantly changing appearances to match up with the subject's true psychological identity; on the other, he is a psychologist, always ascertaining whether to try a direct or nondirect question. He notes facial expressions, eye movement (right eye movement suggests a lying extrovert; left eye, a lying introvert), body English, what isn't said, the tone of what is and nervous habits (e.g., fingers drumming, facial tics).

Despite law enforcement's reliance on the kinesic method, scientific circles look down on this method. Most psychologists believe that much long-range testing needs to be done. Psychologists also warn that interpreting a specific body gesture—usually called a kine—is difficult because the hand to the tip of the nose could indicate real interest or an itchy nose. In other words, is the gesture primarily physiological or psychological?

Confessions. Sometimes the detective shoots for a full admission

A Key to Reading the Body Language of the Interviewee/Suspect

Face: sweat = nervousness

Changes of complexion: extreme (redness, pallid) = nervousness

Adams Apple movement: swallowing = tenseness

Carotid Artery pulsations = nervousness

General Tenseness = stress

Shoulders: hunched, chin to chest, nearly closed eyes = leave me alone; retracted = anger; raised = fear; square = responsible

Repeated fidgeting (with item, running hands through hair, gripping chair, changing positions, tapping feet) = nervousness

Eyes: rapid blinking, avoids contact = liar; lowered = apology; eyebrows raised = interest; long gaze = interest

Mouth: dryness = nervousness; biting fingernails = nervousness

Lips: parted, pout = sexual interest

Smile: broad = friendly; oblong = forced polity

Excessive sweating = nervousness

Arms and fists: crossed = defensive

Hands: clammy = nervous; open = friendly; hidden = guilty; to cheek = pensive; nods head frequently, finger between lips = liar

Legs: ankles locked = withholding information; spread = open; stretched out = shame

Illustration by Tom Post.

and confession. In the movies and TV, stock endings occur when someone breaks down on the stand in a crowded courtroom and admits the murder. In twenty-two years John has never seen anyone confess in open court except those who were going to admit the facts and argue the law. In fact, he doesn't know of one case of spontaneous courtroom confession outside films. It just doesn't happen in real life. By the time suspects reach court, they have become entrenched in their positions and have come under the influence of lawyers.

But confessions do occur at the interview stage. Sometimes they are a complete surprise. The PI is proceeding according to plan when the subject says softly, "You know all about it, don't you?" At this point experienced PIs say nothing and merely pause a beat. Their return looks, though, say, "Of course I do!" Sometimes the detective needs only to prod a bit: "You want to tell me all about it?" Sometimes the subject simply drops the bomb: "I did it." The poor PI may or may not have had a clue that Miss Spontaneous did it, and if the PI had another theory, of course the confession is a shock. Whether or not prepared for the sudden admission, the experienced PI does not register surprise. The jaw locked, the PI proceeds to extract the details from the person who has just gone from subject to full-blown suspect.

John still has nightmares about the time he was interviewing the divorced father of a missing teenage girl named Abbie who was marginally retarded. It was late at night eight miles up Gravel Mountain Road in a lonely, dilapidated shack. John was alone except for the father, who was not considered any kind of suspect by anyone, even the girl's mother (his ex-wife). John was going through the motions just to get the interview out of the way as a formality. He had been in the area on another matter when on impulse he decided to check the girl's father off his "To Do" list. Imagine John's shock, surprise and concern for his personal health when to a routine question about Abbie, the father looked at John with great intensity and mumbled in anguish, "You know'd I did it, don't you?"

"Did what?" replied the ever-sharp John.

"Know I killed her," stated the huge man with tears in his eyes.

Sam Spade might have wisecracked, "I do now, sweetheart." But not John. He was far too cautious—and stunned. Gathering his wits, he spent the next two hours listening to the father rationalize the inexplicable, detailing how he shot Abbie, chopped her up and scattered bits and pieces of her body along the ridges of Gravel Mountain Road.

Detective's M.O. Good detectives are serious students. They study people and books to learn about verbal and nonverbal cues and their meanings. They then adopt and practice modes of speaking and physical actions that best elicit the desired information.

- positioning. The detective sits close to the subject to hear and be heard clearly, but far enough away so as not to encroach upon the interviewee's "space." Recent studies show that people normally become anxious if another person intrudes into a cylindrical area within eighteen inches. The detective moves or removes any intervening object that might hinder direct communication or provide something to hide behind (e.g., large centerpieces on tables, a portable coffeemaker) or distracting objects (e.g., a deck of cards, a child's toy). Such objects can subtly break the psychological rapport the detective has worked so hard to develop. Detectives usually position themselves directly in front of the interviewee so as to observe every bit of facial activity.

- body English. The detective leans forward (signifying interest and concern) as opposed to leaning back in a chair (which appears too casual). The hands are spread wide to suggest openness (as if to say "I have nothing to hide"). The hands are animate ("I am alive and interested in you"), but they make no sudden gestures ("I am threatening you"). The fingers do not drum on the table ("Boy, am I nervous" or "This is boring") nor get in front of the face ("I have something to hide from you"). The shoulders and head move slowly toward the subject ("This is fascinating"), but they don't turn sideways ("I'd rather be in Philadelphia"). In short, every move you make, every breath you take says, "I am interested in you."

- facial expression. Eyelids open. No rapid blinking. Eyes fastened directly on the subject. What psychologists call an open face—no scowls, eyebrows slightly raised, occasional affirmative nod.

- voice. Calm, room temperature (neither too hot nor too cold). No verbal pauses (e.g., hemming, hawing, "You know ..."). Words delivered at moderate pace and clearly enunciated. Language devoid of jargon foreign to interviewee. Diction level, word choice and grammatical patterns match those of interviewee. Tone is informal, nonthreatening, nonjudgmental.

- taboos. Throughout the interview, the detective stays in control and reaches the interview's goal by avoiding certain things:

1. Excessive digressions by either party.

2. Me-isms ("Let me tell you about the time I . . .").

3. Raising the voice/disagreeing with the subject: Personal feelings are for the most part counterproductive. The detective is not there to debate the interviewee.

4. Constant interruptions: The detective must have an unseen hand in steering the conversation on track without appearing irritated or angry.

5. Distracting actions/grooming: B.O. is as bad as picking your nose. Heavy cologne and bad breath kill more conversations than disagreement.

6. Losing concentration: The detective is an active listener; looking away or not thinking about what's being said might cause the PI to miss a key piece of information, to fail to spot the tip of a conversational iceberg, or not to see a significant body gesture (that slightly raised eyebrow, that pause in mid-gulp).

7. Personal thoughts: No matter how attractive the interviewee is, the detective stays focused on business. No matter how touching the subject's story, the detective doesn't think of related personal examples ("My kid started Little League about the same time").

Momentum. An interview in motion must remain in motion. Pauses, distractions and digressions thwart the fact-finding nature of the session. Aside from the previously mentioned matters, most detectives know a few ways to keep the conversation flowing.

1. Vary direct and indirect questions. The PI realizes that simply asking questions becomes repetitive, boring, and can eventually build a barrier between the parties. Sometimes conversations have to wander a bit, like water finding its own level, so that the subject doesn't feel s/he's being led through a series of hoops.

2. Note taking, even when recording, is often a good idea because detectives can emphasize crucial information, draw connec-

tions and jot down notes about what to ask next. Note taking also diverts the subject's attention from hidden recorders. However, detectives have to be careful that the note taking does not distract the subject or cause them to become so engrossed with the words on paper that they miss the meaning of the subject's words.

3. Persistence is important. At some point in an interview the detective feels like a marathon runner "hitting the wall." Keep going. Attack the same point from another direction. Ask and re-ask the questions in different ways.

4. A subject must be led to some extent. Sometimes all it takes is a short phrase of encouragement like "Keep going," "That's it," or "Most people don't have such a good memory for detail." Sometimes it's moving from the known to unknown, the general to the specific ("You said it happened that night. Was it before midnight or after?").

5. "No" doesn't always mean "no." Even when subjects can't or won't answer a question, they may still know the answer. PIs try to determine the reason for verbal shutdown and work around it. Is the subject protecting somebody? Is the subject tired? Did I hit a pressure point (most people have areas they are reticent to talk about to anybody—e.g., a dead child, injuries to animals, sex).

6. Nothing smoothes out the bumps in the conversational road like a good sense of humor.

The Closing

Interviews don't just suddenly end. Still in control, the detective tries to accomplish several goals in the conversation's final moments.

Summarize key information. PIs repeat certain details to make sure they have the specifics correct, always asking the subject if the details are what was said and truly meant. Ambiguities are clarified and explained.

Make the final push. PIs seek out any additional information the subject may wish to add.

Maintain rapport. Practically speaking, the PI may need the interviewee for further questions, depositions, affidavits or even a court appearance. No matter how poorly things have gone, the PI tries to remain upbeat and emphasize the positive ("I'm sorry I took up so much of your time, but I think you've given me some valuable information").

Be cordial. The detective thanks the subject.

Determine whether a written statement is needed. If the subject knows the conversation has been taped, s/he may wish a transcript. Also, if the subject doesn't know the conversation has been recorded, the detective may wish to divulge this information.

Stay alert. The formal part of the meeting over, many subjects voluntarily or involuntarily let down their guard. John has picked up some important information just because he lingered long enough to shake the subject's hand good-bye.

Ask if there is any relevant point that has not been covered in the regular interview. Occasionally subjects will volunteer the most surprising information once they believe the formal interview is ended.

Leave a card. If the subject suddenly remembers something or somebody related to the case contacts him/her, the subject can then notify the PI.

Summary

As in the area of surveillance, you can make your PI more realistic by realizing that successful interviewing is a science with a sophisticated methodology. It demands the detective have a definite purpose for the interview, proper preparation, a well-designed pattern for conducting the interview (including establishing rapport, strategies for moving the interview in the desired direction and closing) and an ability to evaluate the interviewee's verbal and nonverbal responses.

Hints

1. Several major differences exist between interviews by the PI and those by the police. PIs usually have more time and energy to devote to a particular interview, but they can't demand a subject come down to their office.

2. Experts make a distinction between an interview and an interrogation. In the interview the subject may or may not be a suspect; in an interrogation the subject is almost always a suspect or suspected of hiding something. Interviews treat the subject with respect; interrogations treat the suspect more suspiciously.

3. Some interviews are conducted from the beginning with both parties knowing that the conversation will be written up and signed as a formal statement. During the course of an interview or afterwards, a detective may decide the conversation needs to be formalized.

4. Some interviews are conducted over the phone, thus entering a legal mine field. Phone interviews, usually done in an emergency or because of great distance between parties, are less reliable because the detective finds it very difficult to read responses and can't see physical movements. Also, electronic reproduction of speech is not as accurate as our minds tell us. Reporters find that most reporting errors occur in telephone interviews.

5. While we have covered interviews in a single chapter, books have been written on the subject. For one of the best, check out Art Buckwalter's *Interviews and Interrogations*. Buckwalter, a teacher of investigators, provides theory on the art of communicating, written statements, conducting the interview and interrogation problems.

6. Another Landreth Law: Talk is better than silence. Gregarious PIs make the best interviewers. As a character in *The Maltese Falcon* observes, "People like to talk to people who like to talk." John has even been known to talk nonstop to interviewees as a method of intimidating them ("If you'll just shut up, I'll tell you what you want to know").

7. In real life, there are too many clues, too much evidence, too many suspects, too many questions and never enough answers. John stresses that sometimes the case is made by asking the right question to the right person at the right time. Of course, for this principle to work, John has to ask a lot of questions. Why is it, he wonders, that in fiction, PIs (even in panorama) rarely question a subject who is of little or no help and hardly ever ask useless questions?

8. Still another Landreth Law: A PI expects to be lied to. Even people who want to tell the truth often aren't very good at it.

9. Sometimes the most important question is the one the PI *doesn't* ask. Why? Because it may stimulate the subject into doing more than wondering why it wasn't asked.

10. Not all subjects are cooperative. Some are downright hostile. Obviously they must be treated differently.

11. Consider using panorama to cover all the useless interviews, failed leads and talks with people who really know nothing. By providing after-the-fact summations instead of time-consuming scenes, you will create the flavor of the real interview process without boring your readers.

F I F T E E N

PHYSICAL EVIDENCE

As I left the office of the Whoopee Motel, light from the solitary lamppost struck a small object in the parking lot. I probably wouldn't have cared, but the object was lying in the parking space in front of B2. I hurried over and stooped down. It certainly wasn't a bottle cap. The object was a 24-carat gold pin shaped like a giant scythe. I turned it over. An inscription read "TO HD: ALL MY LOVE. LV."

Richard Steele,
Josh Shepherd, PI

What detective story has ever operated without some physical clue or piece of evidence? In the classic locked-room mystery, Holmes or Father Brown always comes upon a significant object that holds the key to a baffling case if only the detective can decipher it ("The solitary fibre I found on the library door handle is Mohair, just like the smoking jacket worn by none other than Major Relish on the night of the murder"). In hard-boiled PI fiction, the physical clue is usually only the first step in a chain of encounters that uncovers the truth of the case. In both cases the detectives often arrive at the scene of the crime after the authorities have fine-tooth combed it.

In real life, detectives encounter loads of clues. They must find each piece of physical evidence, catalog it, examine it and place it within some meaningful scenario—all the while maintaining the tightly linked legal chain of evidence. Remember Pan Am Flight 103 that mysteriously exploded over Lockerbie, Scotland, in 1988? Thousands of investigators combed 845 acres of fields, finding millions of pieces of the once-jumbo jet. Three years later the case broke because of three minute pieces of evidence—two thumbnail-sized electronic circuit boards and a tiny swatch of clothing. By tracing the manufacturers of the boards and clothing, investigators were able to pinpoint the culprits, two Libyan intelligence agents. While a small-town PI could never hope to replicate such an investigation, the principles followed are basically the same.

Types of Evidence

Criminologists and legal scholars generally define evidence as information or objects that help investigators determine what actually happened in a given case. Evidence, the vehicle for establishing all relevant facts, differs from pure information because it has a definite bearing on the outcome of a case. Evidence, then, legally proves or disproves a point in question, but it does not necessarily establish "truth."

Experts usually divide evidence into three major categories: 1) testimony (statements given by a witness), 2) documentary (relating to what a document states and who signed it), and 3) physical evidence. Since the first two categories were examined in part in the preceding chapters on "Interviews" and "Locating Records" (and will be touched upon later in "Law and the Detective"), this chapter concentrates on physical or real evidence.

Physical evidence consists of tangible evidence that can be brought into court to be examined by the judge, jury and attorneys. Truthfully, almost any physical object qualifies, so the category is much larger than most people think. Some of the most common possibilities are weapons, vehicles (often damaged), fibers, possessions (stolen or found at the scene), impressionable objects (from which fingerprints can be lifted, impressions made), stains (notably blood) and fluids (e.g., blood, urine, semen).

A basic quality of physical evidence is that it can be scientifically identified and analyzed. Criminal and forensic laboratories examine such evidence to establish its identity, break down its components and demonstrate linkage to other evidence (e.g., intermingled car paint at an accident).

PIs and the Police

A staple of PI fiction has been that the detective waltzes onto the scene of the crime after the police "lab boys" have supposedly scrutinized it and is still able to discover that all-important "overlooked" clue. In "The Purloined Letter," for instance, the Prefect describes how the Parisian police absolutely *know* the letter in question is hidden somewhere in Minister D's room, yet after a thorough ransacking they have been unable to discover its location. Furniture has been measured for secret drawers, cushions probed with needles, and desks and beds have been disassembled and examined with microscopes. However, Detective Dupin, on a single quick trip to the scene of the crime, easily locates the missing evidence. Which brings up a reasonable question: In real life, can a solitary PI at the scene of the crime discover something vital that the authorities have overlooked?

John answers with an emphatic "Yes" for several reasons. He points out that whether big-city or small-town, law enforcement agencies cannot cope with the ever-growing amount of crime. They are undermanned, overworked and suffering from cut-every-year budgets. With the onslaught of drugs, the police are spread even thinner. If they solve a crime, what is their reward? They have to go to court, which takes time away from solving the next crime. If they do their best to discover evidence and make cases, somewhere along the line a foul-up or worse can result in a blown prosecution. And that generates bad publicity and fault-finding. They get in trouble only for things they do, not for what they don't do. As a result, even the best police have developed what John calls the Frustrated Centurion Attitude.

John also stresses special circumstances. At times physical evidence does not point to where police want the crime to go. For instance, they have a simple solution/obvious suspect before them, but a lone shred of evidence suggests a direction that might take lots of time and much energy to follow to the end. Subconsciously (or even consciously) they "overlook" the conflicting bit of evidence. In other situations they are essentially note takers, report writers. After the first hundred accident investigations, they tend to go on autopilot when they get the 101st, losing all desire to ferret out minute pieces of evidence.

John cites as an example his investigation of a rear-end collision on the interstate between a pickup and a Volkswagen. The state trooper on the scene noted that the major evidence (the pickup's front bumper had the VW's paint embedded in it) made it clear that the VW had been rear-ended. Further on-scene evidence (a breathalyzer test) proved the driver of the pickup had been drinking. Case closed?

Not for John—whose client was the pickup driver. After reading the trooper's report and interviewing him, John returned to the scene of the accident. Still impacted in the guardrail that the VW had taken out was a beer bottle. At a local junkyard John found more of the same brand of beer in the wrecked shell of the VW. When John went back to the trooper, the officer admitted to having seen the beer bottles in the VW but not bothering to put that in his report. John was able to establish the VW driver had been drinking (because he was fatally injured, he was not tested at the accident scene). As a result, John was able to show the VW driver was partially at fault for the accident.

Even in criminal cases (except usually for murder), the police occasionally miss a key piece of physical evidence. A local convenience store was robbed and a female clerk killed. Since the action took place at the cash register area up front, the police concentrated their attention there. When the police investigators turned up no immediate leads, the clerk's family, who knew John, quickly hired him. John has a theory of search he calls the Second Coming Principle that is unlike the traditional grid pattern used by most law enforcement personnel. He begins his search for evidence at the center of the crime, and like the falcon in the Yeats' poem he turns "in an ever-widening gyre [circle]" (John once found a local judge's stolen jewelry in the backyard of the judge's neighbor because the police had stopped their search at the property line). Upon visiting the crime scene, John noticed an overturned soda case at the rear of the store. From the trash on the floor, he knew the mishap must have recently occurred. He looked around, and, sure enough, above him he spotted the dummy video camera the store had installed to scare prospective shoplifters. On closer inspection he realized that someone had stuck a piece of chewing gum over the lens. Further investigation revealed a clear handprint on the surveillance mirror adjacent to the camera. John surmised that the robber(s) had climbed on the soda case to reach the camera and had caught their balance by sticking their hand on the nearby mirror. He was right. Later confronted with the evidence of the palm/fingerprints, the apprehended suspect confessed to the crime and implicated his accomplice. (See illustration next page.)

Search Patterns

"Falcon"   Grid

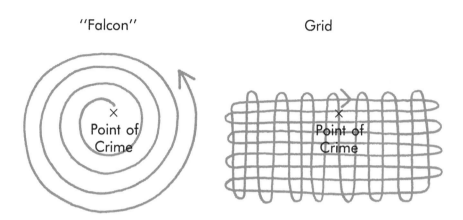

Collecting Evidence

The day is long past when the private inquiry agent (an old name for the PI) wandered around the country estate, occasionally pausing to stare through a large magnifying glass and mutter, "Hmmm!" So what does today's PI actually do at the crime scene and how does that procedure differ from the police?

Whether the case is locating a missing person, an accident investigation or solving a robbery, John has a general M(odus) O(perandi) he likes to follow. He finds that his evolved-over-time standard operating procedure gives him the best chance to understand the situation, know the people involved and perhaps find a piece of relevant physical evidence.

Visit the scene ASAP. After the initial interview with his client, John likes to proceed to the scene of the crime/accident. In the pickup collision case, had he not gone to the exact spot on the interstate immediately, rain might have washed away the bottle, the state might have repaired the guardrail, and the trooper might have forgotten what he hadn't put into his report. Moreover, the VW might have been crushed into a paperweight or the driver's family might have thought to get the beer bottles out of the car. At the convenience store, had he waited another hour, the owner might have cleaned up the soda boxes, and John would never have gotten close enough to see the palm print on the surveillance mirror.

As an ex-cop, John is very much aware he is not the police. In PI fiction when detectives visit the crime scene, they often appear to be running the investigation or, at the very least, "one of the boys" privy to all the police find. In real life, if John arrives at the scene before the police (and friends have called him before the cops), John knows not to touch anything, but to secure the area. Of course, while he is doing this, he observes carefully. If he arrives while the police are there, he usually finds himself treated with less respect than that accorded a family member. If he's done his job throughout the years and cultivated friends in uniform, John might be allowed to stay as an observer (once again, it doesn't pay to make enemies of the local gendarmes). Mostly, though, he's looked upon as a nosy neighbor, a nuisance, and he rarely has a cop saunter up to him and say, "Hey, good buddy, let me fill you in on what we've found." If John arrives after the police have left, he often encounters the familiar yellow tape securing the scene, but usually he has free access to the area fairly quickly.

Soak up the environment. At the very least, John wants to get a feel for the situation. If nothing else, he learns all he can about his client. But mostly he likes to survey the area for things other people (friends, relatives, parents, children, the police) think insignificant.

Once John was working a missing person's case. The first thing he noticed on visiting the lost teenager's room was books galore. The kid was a reader. Especially of comic books. And stacked neatly in long cardboard boxes in the closet was a collection of comic books, each one in a protective plastic sleeve. During the interview the kid's mother (John's client) had never thought to mention that her son liked to read comics. His reading was so commonplace to her that she hadn't bothered to bring it up. Within a month John traced the noncustodial father, whom he suspected responsible, to a large city in the deep South. There, John showed the boy's photo to the owner of a local comic book specialty shop (looked up in the Yellow Pages), which led John to the boy. Dupin was right when he claimed, "Perhaps it is the very simplicity of the thing which puts you at fault."

In the environment John feels he has one edge over the police—he cares. It may be the police investigator's fiftieth childnapping, and he's going to get paid whether he solves the crime or not. For John, it's first blood.

Look for the unusual. That Holmes-boy of detectives, Sherlock, once noted in *Silver Blaze* that what was unusual one night was that the dog *didn't* bark. John recalls a burglary case wherein he noticed that next to the spot where the television set had been was a shelf of toy soldiers. John, a collector himself, spotted something peculiar. One of the 30mm Hessians was out of formation. With a guess and a little dust, John brought out a fingerprint that eventually drew a match and solved the case. Evidently, the burglar had been curious and picked up the toy soldier.

Keep records of what you find. A good PI is handy with a camera. Lots of John's colleagues are all too ready to take pictures of dead bodies — and live ones through seedy motel curtains. But John realizes the importance of photography with physical evidence. Usually when he arrives upon the scene, he takes a few "establishing shots" to use later if for nothing other than to refresh his memory. He knows, too, he will sometimes notice a relevant detail in a photo that he didn't see when he was at the scene. Moreover, John always takes some shots of specific physical evidence he uncovers (both a close-up and a composition shot to reveal its location relative to other objects in the scene). John takes notes (either with pencil or tape), carefully noting dates, times, witnesses.

Often John finds one piece of physical evidence is unimportant until it's juxtaposed to another. In one rape case he read a transcript wherein the suspect's reasoning was "I couldn't have raped her. Any time she wanted she could have left through the rear door." Sensing something wrong with the man's story, John got out his pictures of where the alleged rape had taken place. Sure enough, John was right. The room in question didn't have a back door. The most unusual piece of photographic evidence? John once had to make a close-up photograph of a prisoner to be able to prove in court the man had been circumcised.

Recognize your limits. John realizes he is no more a lab technician than a policeman. Unlike Sherlock Holmes, John cannot look at a person's mud-caked boots and immediately know in which part of the county the man has been lately. And the only magnifying glass he carries is to read small print. He rarely picks up guns with the pencil-in-the-barrel trick (which is a good way to get shot) or uses

Missing Links: John's Crimeboard

To help him solve a case, John finds he needs to create perspective—to step back from the immediate and see the big picture. Sometimes (on his basement office wall) he tapes cards that represent the major players. Then, as he spots relationships between them, he joins those cards with string. What looks like contemporary kinetic art gone awry to the outsider becomes meaningful to John. John then puts the whole thing down on paper and writes in relationships.

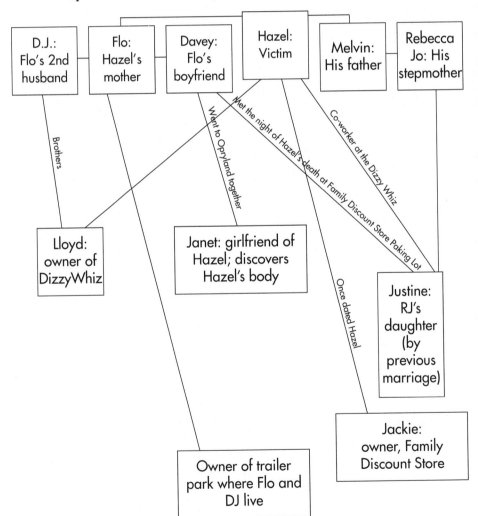

tweezers to snatch up hairs. And he doesn't carry baggies in his jacket to gather fibers. John may have an interesting home, but it's not equipped with a laboratory for testing bloodstains and exotic poisons. Only on rare moments has he pointed out palm prints on surveillance mirrors to the police. Occasionally he has sent off paint samples to private laboratories to be analyzed. He's very careful neither to contaminate nor mutilate any evidence.

Rotten Apple—The Turncoat

When this rotten apple uncovers evidence, his client does not always benefit. Often the client's problems have just begun. The turncoat is essentially a mercenary whose loyalties are not with the client, but with the green. The turncoat will start out on one side of a case—say, Side A—uncover something on Side B, and offer to sell it to B for more than A is paying. A favorite variant of this game is "use the client." PIs usually look into a client's background before they take the case. So, suppose A hires P.T. Shamus to investigate B. As a matter of course, Shamus checks out A, uncovers some dirt and offers it to B. Or, Shamus might decide to hold an auction, working both sides of the street for a fistful of dollars, selling out not to just the highest bidder, but selling both sides to both sides.

Chain of Evidence

A familiar TV scene occurs when the green lawyer admits to the judge that a warrant was improperly served, that a police search was blatantly illegal, or that the search extended beyond the scope of the warrant. Thus, the evidence is tainted, hence inadmissible, and the suspect is "cut loose." Why does this never happen to a PI? In truth, private investigators must be as careful as the police in finding, cataloging, identifying and presenting evidence.

Courts are always concerned with the possibility of tainted evidence—that it was illegally obtained or tampered with in transit to trial. While not all evidence the PI finds will eventually show up in court, the PI must treat every piece as though it will. Hence, good notes, as John previously stated, become essential in establishing where, when and by whom the evidence was found, as well as who else might have handled it (e.g., laboratories) on its way to court.

Manufacturing Evidence

Not all evidence shows up in court and, thus, isn't subject to the same legal scrutiny. John remembers a case where a man called him early one evening, and wanted him to grab a camera and meet him outside a local motel. When John got there, the client explained that he had suspected his wife of infidelity and had followed her to the motel; at that very moment she was inside with her lovers, two women, and he wanted John to get some incriminating photos. Unfortunately, though he had a nice view into the hotel room, John had brought neither night film nor an infrared camera, so it looked like the opportunity was lost.

Not really. The next night John returned with three actresses, rented the same motel room, had them pose in positions he remembered from the previous night, and shot the whole thing with a camera, deliberately creating blurred, barely visible photos. The reproduced photos got John's client a divorce and custody of his young kids, as well as producing two other divorces.

The key for John was the bluff, but even so, he notes that cops sometimes, out of frustration, manufacture evidence. One of the great pieces of evidence in a courtroom is fingerprints. Yet, John has seen cops use tape to lift a suspect's prints off of one object (say, a coffee cup) and put them on another (say, a vial of cocaine). He knows of cops who have deliberately taken fibers and dust samples from a burglar's car and planted them on seized stolen merchandise — "salting the mine." In real life even "good" cops and PIs stretch the limits of the law occasionally. It's up to you as the writer to fit this reality into your PI's code of ethics.

In his days as a cop John once found a truck out of gas near the scene of an armed robbery. After obtaining the home address of the truck's owner, the police went to the house. The suspect said he'd been home all day, his truck had been stolen from in front of his house the night before and his live-in girlfriend backed up his story. As the man was in the bathtub when the police arrived, John spotted the man's pants draped over a chair. He surreptitiously purloined the suspect's wallet. Later in the interview John asked the man if he hadn't been at the scene of the crime, then how come they'd found his wallet there. The suspect immediately confessed to the robbery.

Summary

To be credible, your PI must know what constitutes valid evidence in a case, how to uncover this evidence, how to collect it, label it, establish a proper (and legal) chain of evidence to insure the evidence's admissibility in court.

Hints

1. Evidence, physical or otherwise, is a legal concept. Many books have been written on the subject from a legal perspective alone. Art Buckwalter's *The Search for Evidence* is a thorough treatise on evidence from an investigator's viewpoint. Although much of Buckwalter's advice is aimed more at police investigators, he still covers types and rules of evidence, witnesses and written, physical and photographic evidence. Moreover, he has a bibliography detailing all sorts of specialties (e.g., arson investigation, principles of photography).

2. Local labs can tell you what tests they are capable of performing and supply you with a price list.

3. Since all the evidence the PI collects will not make it to court, the PI does not always have to think like a lawyer. Detectives have been known to use illegally obtained evidence to pressure subjects in noncourt-approved manners. For instance, while hearsay evidence is inadmissible in court, it can be used in interviews to pry information out of subjects.

4. Place some credence in the single-clue theory. While most cases involve many clues, some pieces of physical evidence are more important than others. Many times the PI's tracing of a solitary shred of evidence from start to finish leads to a breakthrough. Most detectives don't know how important a particular clue is until after it's traced and the results are known.

5. Make your detective a shutterbug. Even if s/he carries a Brownie Hawkeye camera left over from childhood, have your PI take a lot of pictures. Detectives don't trust their memory.

They shoot a lot of film, develop it and mark on the rear the time, location and angle. John often takes shots in pairs; the first one is a "natural" and the second is basically the same shot with a ruler in it (thus giving a sense of real proportion and size).

6. Detectives notice detail the way mom always knew where to find that missing pair of shoes. The power of observation is a common trait that you should set up early in your story. Try to give as much description as possible from the PI's point of view, including many precise details. This technique creates the impression of your detective as meticulous observer.

7. Stay current with technological advances. Too much PI fiction uses earlier PI fiction for its sources. For instance, paraffin tests to detect the presence of nitrates on the suspect's hand after the firing of a gun have been replaced by more complex and reliable equipment. And fingerprints can be spotted on corpses with an ingenious new device that emits green light, rendering the prints visible.

8. Detectives make rough sketches of crime/accident scenes. Most new police forms even come with part of the sketch begun. John likes to draw fairly precise sketches of such scenes. Pictures are nice, but they don't show height, width, length or distance.

9. How much physical evidence is enough? John always tries to collect enough so that he can reconstruct an accident or crime. Once he even re-created the robbery of a convenience store by using the actual location and local actors, shooting the action in dim light and slightly out of focus. His results were so accurate that when he showed the videotape to the driver of the getaway car, John was able to convince him that he had filmed the accomplices during the actual robbery. The driver confessed.

10. Check out two of the previous books in the Howdunit series. Both *Cause of Death* and *The Scene of the Crime* provide a detailed look at the collection of evidence. In the latter, Anne Wingate offers insight into the nature of fingerprints, how human remains are identified and evidence collection. In the former, Dr. Keith Wilson details how physical evidence is used to determine whether a death was by accident or intention.

HIRED HELP

*I was beginning to feel like a screwed-up compass. This case was
pointing me in too many different directions. As much as Josh Shepherd
hated to admit it, he needed help. And there was only one person to
call. I picked up my cellular phone and dialed Daius X. Macheena. The
X stood for a lot of things — ex-cop, ex-football player and ex-chemistry
teacher. He had pulled my fat out of the fire more than once, and right
now I needed a man with asbestos hands.*

Richard Steele,
Josh Shepherd, PI

In PI fiction, when detectives are backed into a dark corner, too
often as a last resort they turn to a specialist, that one person with
the particular ability to help them ferret out the truth or perform
that essential task needed to solve the case. Sometimes these experts
are forensic scientists (i.e., cut-rate Quincys in lab coats who perform needed tests either for free, friendship or a cold one), brute
forces (look no further than Parker's Hawk), computer technicians
(aka The Hacker) or the Friend on the Force (who supplies forbidden knowledge about a current case). At times like this, PIs seem
to have their own I(mpossible)M(issions)F(orce) on call.

In truth, even real-life small-town PIs do not stalk those mean
streets all by themselves all the time. Occasionally they need help —
sometimes to complete their investigations, sometimes to get
through daily tasks they aren't equipped to handle or sometimes to
wrap up a case. In real life, these people reside in the PI's Rolodex.

Basic Support

As discussed in an earlier chapter, a secretary is nice but nonessential. PIs can learn to type and hire answering services. In real life, having a secretary necessitates an office, paying Social Security, meeting a biweekly payroll and worrying whether the secretary won't be able to come into work because of sickness, death or vacation time. Often two PIs will work out of the same office and share a secretary (who also often functions as surrogate mother). Often, too, that secretary is a spouse or significant other.

An accountant/CPA is almost always necessary for the PI, especially if the PI has a secretary. Government forms, taxes and payrolls must be handled, and most PIs, though they are in actuality small businesspersons, don't have a business mentality.

Throughout this book we've touched upon the relationship of the PI and the lawyer from starting-up contracts to court appearances. Because PIs often operate on the edge of the law, they end up in court testifying, and since this is a litigious society, it helps a PI to have a friend who is an attorney. Usually it's a quid pro quo relationship, a barter system whereby the lawyer looks over contracts for the PI and the PI does a little investigative work every now and then. One common fear of PIs that even Stephen King hasn't written about is IRS-phobia, but most PIs realize that even the federal government dislikes pursuing clients of lawyer-accountants.

Part-Time Operatives

Small-town PIs working alone usually have a cadre of part-timers who are readily available. Such PIs most often don't have sufficient business to keep their help busy full time, but since business comes in fits and starts, it is comforting to know the part-timer is there.

Ed Hino of Lansdale, Pennsylvania, has two part-timers, both former law enforcement agents. These licensed part-timers are "on call," and Ed uses them whenever his caseload gets heavy or he is unavailable or doesn't want to take the job. Mostly, Ed sends his people to interview accident witnesses and to perform background checks on job applicants.

Most states require part-timers to be licensed. Still, many PIs use unlicensed help — often off-duty cops — for simple work such as surveillance or guard duty.

Specialists

Real-life PIs cultivate relationships with people in areas they may need before they actually need such experts. A cold call to a name in the Yellow Pages doesn't bring quick results — unless a little extra cash is thrown in.

Photographers. Courtroom pictures must be well focused, clear and well composed. Everyday snaps of crime/accident scenes are not the best evidence. Moreover, if the PI accompanies the photog to the scene, in court PIs can produce the key photograph, the shooter and themselves. Corroborated evidence is very effective.

Off-Duty Police. PIs occasionally make use of cops. By employing their expertise and abilities — often as security in protecting persons or sites — detectives help their clients and build good relationships with the police, who are being paid for their efforts. Sometimes off-duty cops make good consultants. With a fire of suspicious origin, the PI might desire the knowledge of a local arson investigator; in a shooting, a cop who knows weaponry.

Graphologists. Hoover's FBI swore by handwriting experts. Not only could they authenticate documents, signatures, etc., but they also could analyze a subject's handwriting to determine personality traits. John has used graphologists to authenticate whether letters were actually written by a supposed missing person and often to analyze an adversary's personality to understand why the subject had done what s/he had done.

Electronics. Remember, PIs never wiretap; they engage in electronic countersurveillance measures. Semantics aside, detectives often need such specialists. In divorce cases, for instance, in states where it is legal to tap your own phone, detectives have used experts to bug the phones of spouses who fear they are being cheated on by their significant other. High tech specialists often do nothing but continuously debug corporate headquarters.

Criminals. Poe's Dupin claimed the way to solve crimes was for the detective to identify his/her intellect with that of the perpetrator. To get inside the head of a burglar, John has been known to talk to another B&E specialist about vulnerable points of entry, useful tools, ways of canvassing a target, etc. Moreover, John has used con artists and pimps to obtain desirable ends (see chapter seventeen on "Making It Happen").

Contacts and Informants

Contacts and informants are hired help, but they overlap some of the previous categories (e.g., police). A contact is a person in power who is privy to particular information sought by the PI. Potential contacts, therefore, exist in almost every relevant field from law enforcement (local to federal level) to insurance, from government work to private industry, from businesspersons to day laborers. John has found that contacts will help him for various reasons. Some have an axe to grind, some may want to borrow John's axe one day and some need money to pay for their own axe. Some actually seek John out; others John goes after because of the nature/scope of a particular case. For instance, because John does a lot of work with kids in trouble (runaways, kidnapped), he likes having friends in area child welfare offices. Another of Landreth's Laws is that contacts are like tobacco; they've got to be cultivated before they can be harvested. The best contacts? Best changes from case to case, but as a rule the higher they are in their respective hierarchy, the greater the info they have access to.

While contacts may break the law by supplying the PI with supposedly forbidden knowledge, informants start out on the other side of the law. Police develop informants because the majority of crimes solved results from details supplied by snitches. Thus, some snitches are kept on a regular payroll. Such informants are rarely worthwhile for private investigators. PIs get involved with crimes and civil procedures usually committed by people who are not notorious criminals. Occasionally relatives, ex-spouses and people who know the victim will snitch on the perpetrator to John. Sometimes, as in divorce cases, John has so many snitches he has conflicting information. Usually snitches give out information to the police for money/protection. John finds the informants he deals with have more personal and emotional reasons—such as revenge. A major problem with such snitches is that they often lie; their desire to get back at somebody overrides their willingness to tell the truth. As a result, John spends a lot of time checking out their stories.

Role-Players

Actors. While not all PIs employ actors, John finds that actors can help provide solutions to difficult cases. Once, in Cincinnati, John had to hire an actress to pose as his pregnant wife so that he could get close to the noncustodial parent of a kidnapped child. In another noncustodial childnapping case, John tracked the mother from Kentucky to New Hampshire, where she and a new live-in boyfriend were renting a house. Worried about the child's safety because the boyfriend had a history of violence, John decided that before snatching the little boy away, he had to determine if the boyfriend had a weapon. That meant getting close. So John hired an actress to pose as his wife. Then under the guise of buying the house, the happy "couple" got a real estate agent to show it to them. While the boyfriend was checking out the very good-looking actress, John checked out the house, determining the boyfriend kept a loaded handgun beside him most of the time. John has also hired women to pretend to be Avon ladies to surveil a house he couldn't get near without drawing attention to himself.

Cabdrivers. Since cabs can go most anywhere, they are rarely suspicious. John has paid drivers to surveil areas for him and has even posed as a driver a few times. Once, to determine if a suspected philandering husband was really going on a business trip, John arranged to be the cabbie who picked him up (i.e., paid big bucks to the cabbie entering the subdivision). No sooner had the businessman jumped in the cab than he gave John an address that wasn't the local airport. It turned out to be the apartment of the businessman's girlfriend. Unfortunately, John sighs, cabdrivers and cabs themselves aren't too common in the eastern Kentucky mountains.

Prostitutes. Raymond Chandler suggested the best key for a PI to unlock any door was a hundred-dollar bill. John thinks it's a woman. He recalls a case where a local bank teller ran off with a department store buyer, and in leaving she took her son. Unfortunately, she didn't have custody of him, so her ex-husband hired John to find the boy. John located the couple in Arizona and quickly determined the boy wasn't going anywhere without his mother. So the trick became to convince the woman to leave on her own. In searching their premises one day, John discovered her boyfriend had a collection of Oriental pornography. Then, through surveillance, John learned that the man, now a shoe salesman, liked to tape the ex-teller's eyes into slants a la Oriental women. John devised a plan, but when he couldn't find a local Oriental prostitute, he had to go to San Francisco and import one for a thousand dollars. He then sent her into the Arizona shoe store. The boyfriend quickly sized up her foot, and invited her to lunch and then some sex. When John showed the photos of the afternoon delight to the ex-bank teller, she was convinced to return to Kentucky.

The boyfriend in the New Hampshire custody kidnapping case was also resolved with a prostitute. Unable to persuade New Hampshire authorities to recognize an Ohio court order, John knew he had to get the boyfriend off the scene. The actress-wife was sent home and a prostitute located. John moved her into an apartment near the boyfriend's house. Pretty soon the boyfriend came by to chat with his bikini-clad neighbor. She suggested a weekend in Canada. He bit. When they got there, she drugged his drink. John walked in, fired off a few rounds with a pistol, placed the gun in the happily sleeping boyfriend's hand and called the Canadian police. John had an easy time getting the child back to his father.

Others

Domestics. John is an equal opportunity employer. Not only does he make use of specialists at the top of their profession, but he also employs a variety of blue-collar workers. Janitors, maids, servers and busboys—because they are invisible in our culture—can get close to people without being noticed, have access to rooms and diners and can procure various articles. John has used these people to bring him a water glass with a subject's fingerprints on it, to let him into a hotel room and to eavesdrop on a dinner tête-à-tête. They have searched people's suitcases for him and brought him the contents of wastebaskets (John also holds an advanced degree in garbology, believing that what people throw away tells him as much about them as what they keep). To get closer to a subject, John has posed as a janitor, a limo driver and a bellman.

Another of Landreth's many laws: What's good for the hound is good for the fox. If he can use some of the aforementioned tactics against others, obviously, John reasons, they can use them against him. Over the years he has developed a healthy paranoia concerning hired help. Temp secretaries and even new janitors in his building arouse his suspicions. And since he has a habit of lunching at Frisch's, he's careful not to talk to clients about confidential matters if he notices a server or a busboy hovering around.

Is this paranoia unfounded? A few years ago he was working

on a sticky divorce case. He and his wife returned early from a dinner and caught a longtime babysitter going through his file on the case. She had been bought off by the other side. John never ceases to be amazed at how often true-blue friends can be turned by the color green.

Wannabes. Rock stars have groupies, basketball players have hoopies and modern-day Dupins have "Dupies." Such detective wannabes can be useful and some, a pain in the rump. Hardly a week goes by that John isn't contacted by somebody wanting to serve as his unpaid apprentice.

Throughout his career John has operated with partners and has used wannabes in less dangerous cases. A few years ago a sociology professor who lived across the street from John kept bugging him to tag along on a trip down those mean streets. Eventually the prof wore down John's resistance. So John, needing temp help, let him share the driving down to Florida (some sixteen hours) to pick up a bailjumper. The hardest part of the case for John was fending off the professor's constant questions about John's "plan" for locating and capturing the skip. John couldn't explain that a lot of time with routine investigations he plays it by ear. They drove into Frostproof, located the skip and cuffed him. When it was over, all the professor could do was shake his head and mutter, "One hour and nineteen minutes."

And then there was the time these two profs came to John with their plan about writing a book on what a real-life PI does . . .

Summary

When your PI needs hired help, you should be familiar with what's available in terms of basic support (secretary, accountant, lawyer), part-time operatives, specialists (e.g., photographers, electronics experts), contacts (e.g., police, government workers, criminals), even actors. Each of these "helpers" must be dealt with differently to achieve desired results.

Hints

1. If hired help is necessary to aid your detective, especially close to solution time, introduce that character's existence early in

the story. Don't make the specialist seem to have suddenly materialized on the spot.

2. Make your PI's relationship with hired help believable. Some help can be friends; some, not. Very few people, even good friends, work for nothing. If your detective must use an electronics or graphics expert, make a point of compensation (and make it more than doughnuts and old debts for data). If the help should be licensed and isn't, have the PI aware of breaking the law (or if the PI's not aware of the pertinent law, that omission could be part of the plot).

MAKING IT HAPPEN

*I looked away from the gloom of my cluttered office. I was stuck, sty-
mied, at an impasse. Suddenly I remembered the words of a small-town
PI I had known in Kentucky. "A good detective is a catalyst. It is not
always what he does that's important, but rather what he causes others
to do just by his presence in the case." Landreth's Law, number 101,
he had called it. "Sometimes you have to simply make it happen by
bringing everything to a boil because things don't explode or even break
at room temperature. A PI can't always be a bonfire or even a campfire
under the kettle, but he can at least be a match."*

*By my thinking of something else entirely, inspiration struck. I picked
up the phone and dialed Mr. Euripides's private number. When he answered, I began to lie — earnestly.*

Richard Steele,
Josh Shepherd, PI

In chemistry, a catalyst is a substance that causes a reaction when
mixed with other substances, but by itself remains unchanged. Its
major purpose is to speed up the reaction of the other chemicals.
In the day-to-day world, successful detectives are catalysts. In an
investigation they can cause reactions on the part of the other individuals involved. While these reactions may vary widely from person
to person, they are somewhat predictable and controllable to an
experienced hand.

For instance, in a murder case in which the killer is not known,
the police may be on the lookout for someone who doesn't like to
be approached or questioned and will react in a certain pattern of
behavior that the guilty often affect. John remembers once talking
to the husband of a missing woman. The man, Roy, who was not
John's client, should have been delighted to have a PI of John's
reputation working to find the wayward wife. He wasn't. In fact,
after the first contact, he refused to be interviewed further, even by
the police.

To the experienced investigator, the husband's strange behavior was a red flag. And indeed the husband had murdered his wife and hidden her body under a corn crib in the barn. John's questions about her during the interview had so alarmed him that he refused to see the police, wouldn't talk to anybody and hired an attorney. These were hardly the actions of a loving, innocent husband. While his silence did not prove him guilty, it did suggest to John and to the police where to concentrate their efforts as well as what to ignore — the husband's red herrings.

Stirring Things Up

The old detective-movie cliché about villains tripping themselves up while trying to outwit the PI does have some basis in fact. An investigator often simply stirs up the simmering pot, causing the people involved to collide and bounce off each other, interacting, reacting, ricocheting until something breaks.

For instance, in the aforementioned case, the husband-murderer was entrenched and unapproachable by both John and the police, who did not have sufficient evidence for an arrest even after the wife's body was found three months later. Blocked by the main suspect's stonewalling, John located a different angle of attack. Approaching the grown daughter of the victim and the killer, John convinced her that she could help get to the bottom of things. Because she could come and go at her father's house, the site of the murder, she was able to talk to her younger brothers and sisters at home, who knew things the father was hiding from everyone else. As often happens, in the end the father's attempts to convince his daughter of his innocence tripped him up. He gave her a story that was subsequently disproved, proving his guilt.

Prodding the Suspect

Indirect prodding of a suspect is one of John's favorite techniques. On one occasion he knew from experience that a murderer's lawyer was himself a greedy criminal. So John made sure he was seated next to the lawyer at a political fund-raiser and drew him into a talk-shop conversation. Then, between the so-so roast beef and the au jus, John let slip that he knew the killer had pigeonholed some $35,000 to be used if he were indicted. John even divulged to the attorney where the money was banked and under what name, but he was careful to emphasize that the killer would use this money only if indicted. Suddenly the lawyer, who had been highly successful in keeping his client unindicted, had a vested interest in seeing that client charged and indicted—which he was. After two hung juries and two mistrials, though, the killer walked free, acquitted. But the killer was also unburdened of $35,000 and his farm. Furthermore, John notes, people branded as killers are rarely truly innocent in the eyes of the public, so if the scales of justice can't be perfectly balanced, they can at least be tilted in the right direction.

Prodding, then, begins with the detective discovering the right prime mover for the subject. The ruse is subsequently geared to take advantage of that character weakness—e.g., greed, lust, jealousy. Ed Hino likens this process to akido, the martial arts discipline that uses opponents' momentum to defeat them.

Direct Catalyst

While often a PI is an indirect catalyst whose mere presence in a case causes people to respond, a good PI will not always count on that alone to bring things to a head. Sometimes the PI must become a direct, voluntary, intentional catalyst to make it happen.

This is not to say that the police never use this tactic. An undercover investigation such as a drug buy is a good example of making it happen. So too is a sting where the police pose as fences, buying back stolen property and dealing directly with perps over an extended period of time. But these two ruses are the exception rather than the rule. Even if the cops fail miserably, they still draw their biweekly pay. PIs, unlike the police, are under pressure to be successful in every case; if they develop a reputation for failure—even mediocrity—they may not have many future jobs.

So how do PIs make it happen?

Any way they can.

The Honey Pot

Some tricks are as old as history. The Bible tells of Joshua sending spies to scope out Jericho and infiltrators to spread false rumors through the ranks of the enemy. David ordered Bathsheba's husband into battle to facilitate death and widowhood. John points out that among the oldest "gags" is the "honey pot," which derives from the old hunter's practice of using a pot of honey to bait a bear trap.

To the police there are two kinds of entrapment—legal and illegal. In reality, they practice both, but in court they claim to have only used the legal kind. For the PI, entrapment comes in two types—the good kind (that works) and the bad kind (that fails). For instance, if Mrs. Plum thinks Colonel Plum has a wandering eye and is seeing other women, she may hire a PI whose best course may be to put strange women in the Colonel's usual path. The rest is up to the Colonel.

This technique has become one of John's favorite ways of making it happen. A few years ago, for instance, a wealthy father hired John to investigate his prospective son-in-law, who turned out to be a first-class rotter and a second-class gold digger. The bride-to-be, though, was too smitten to believe conventional proof, so John arranged a meeting between one of his best female operatives and the future groom. This would have been a pretty standard operation except for the profession of the wandering hubby-to-be; he was a funeral director. So the prostitute went to the potential son-in-law, telling him that her cat had died and if he would embalm it, she would be ever so grateful. Things ran their course, and the prostitute even managed to videotape her dalliance in the back room of the funeral parlor with the would-be son-in-law. The hardcore pictures were enough to turn the client's wedding march into a funeral dirge for the undertaker's ambitions.

The honey pot can be many enticements. John once hired a woman to canvas a small neighborhood, giving away coupons for a bargain baby portrait. The coupons, which John had printed up, entitled each bearer to a free box of Gerber's baby food and a photo for a dollar. Those people who brought their kids to the announced location got everything promised—except for a lady who had kidnapped her own infant son and was hiding out in a rural robbers' roost in southern West Virginia, where even the local authorities feared to go, much less involve themselves in a custody fight. After all, this was the land of the Hatfields and McCoys. John rented a special studio room at the local Holiday Inn.

While waiting for the baby to be photographed, John's female operative let it slip to the mother that she was looking to hire a replacement for herself so she could accept a recent promotion. The mom bit so hard she swallowed the honey—pot and all. Momentarily leaving the baby in the capable hands of John the photographer, she departed with the female operative for a free lunch and a chance to discuss this golden opportunity. The minute the mother was out the door, the child's father—John's client, who had full legal custody— stepped out of the bathroom, served his custody papers on John and departed with the child. Conveniently John recorded the whole transaction on videotape to show no custodial interference or kidnapping occurred on his part. The mother returned to find a letter informing her that the baby had been returned to the father.

Expensive Tricks

Sometimes making it happen costs a lot of money. But a good PI has to be willing to invest time and money in a sting. Once in New Hampshire John agreed to buy a house and gave the agent $1,000 in earnest money (the money was nonreturnable and ultimately lost in the caper). As a result, though, another custody kidnapper, a father who happened to be living with a local cop, had to move out and into a location more susceptible to John's favorite method of attack. Soon the father was living in an apartment and, during the day while the cop was away, was making ends meet with his new, sexy neighbor (planted by John). She suggested the old weekend trip to Canada ploy. At the border the authorities found guns and drugs in his suitcase (they actually belonged to the mark, but he didn't know they had been packed and brought along). He was arrested, and the mother, who just happened to be standing there with California custody papers, was given the child.

Such ploys are uncommon. For them to work, the detective must be able to 1) determine how much the client wants results, 2) ascertain how much the client is willing to pay for the ruse and its props, and 3) figure out the specific ruse that will bring the desired result.

More Routine Ruses

Not all John's ruses are so major or flamboyant. Recently John was hired by a tire company to recover some heavy equipment tires that had been paid for with a local wildcatter's check that subsequently bounced. With ten tires worth $8,000 a piece at stake, John took his time surveying the lay of the land. Then, posing as another wildcatter, John rented the heavy earthmover from the wildcatter and had it delivered to a remote strip mine site. When the owner returned to pick up the equipment, it was there all right, but it sat on concrete blocks—tireless. The check for John's rental fee was good, but the deposit check bounced.

This simple ruse worked because of the wildcatter's obvious lack of scruples and the inexpensive nature of the ploy. The detective must fit the ruse to the situation, the client and the "mark."

Really Making It Happen

John considers cases for insurance companies prime candidates for the direct catalyst approach. In part, this is because John has developed a reputation for making it happen. A case in point. A month before they would be forced to pay, an insurance company hired John to prove that an injured man was faking a major neck and spinal problem. Hurt in an accident, he was suing because the injuries prevented him from performing his matrimonial duties. Early attempts to entice the neckbrace-wearing con artist had been unsuccessful because the man's wife watched over her husband's activities like a mother hen.

John's initial investigation determined that Mr. Neckbrace was only allowed to go fishing without her if he went with his next-door crony. They often drove from their home in Dayton, Ohio, to Lake Cumberland in southern Kentucky to fish for the weekend. John could never get close enough, though, to prove the suer, once in the fishing boat, took the neckbrace off.

On one trip John noticed Neckbrace fill out a contest form for a free weekend in one of the resort's houseboats. A few days later, his preparations in place (read "bribe" to the resort officials), John had a woman call and inform Neckbrace that he was the winner. As expected, he and neighbor Harry showed up—without the wives—for the free weekend.

On arriving, the two adventurers were pleasantly surprised to find that the boat came complete with a well-stocked bar and a crew of beautiful women—a redheaded maid, a brunette hostess and a blonde bartender. The friendly female crew (missing from the streets of Louisville that weekend) encouraged inhibitions and clothes to drop like leaves in autumn.

John carefully videotaped the weekend to verify the suee had removed the neckbrace and didn't need its services. The tapes further displayed the erstwhile Mr. Brace waterskiing, highdiving off the roof of the houseboat and swinging a la Tarzan from a rope and dropping into the lake. Mr. Brace was also fully able to perform his male role—with the bartender, the hostess and the maid.

Summary

To make your PI an aggressive problem-solver, you should become acquainted with the strategies used by real-life detectives to shake up the situation in a static case and make things happen. PIs prod suspects by playing upon their weaknesses (e.g., greed, lust, jealousy) and creating ruses (some simple, some complex) that take advantage of these individual weaknesses and draw subjects into damning actions.

Hints

1. If you choose to have your PI perform similar ruses, you must endow him/her with the mental capacity to do so. In simple terms, this means that early in the work you must prepare your reader to accept such efforts. Remember how Conan Doyle began so many of Holmes's stories with the Great Detective demonstrating his mental acumen to Watson?

2. Try to keep the ruse within the client's ability to pay. Only the IMF—and we don't mean the International Monetary Fund—has unlimited funds. Do you think a down-and-out PI could afford to berth an expensive yacht at the Bar Harbor Yacht Club to carry out a scam for a deserving but destitute single parent in a child custody case?

3. Ruses must be fitted to the mark. If the mark is a blue-collar worker whose idea of heaven is a pool room and a Pabst Blue Ribbon, you don't want to fashion a scam involving a five-star restaurant. That's not credible.

4. Research the viability of the scam. Would it really work given the laws of human nature and physical science? Can an individual's backyard satellite dish really intercept military intelligence signals being bounced off geostationary satellites?

THE REPORT

I'd been in the business longer than McDonald's had been hustling Big Macs, and the part of it I hated the most wouldn't stop preying on my mind. I'd rather slug it out with Mike Tyson or shoot it out with the Iraqi Army than do paperwork. Writing the report to Carolyn that night took me nine hours — one-half hour to jot down a few bits and pieces about old Phil and seven and one-half hours to get drunk enough to start jotting.

Richard Steele,
Josh Shepherd, PI

The game's not over till the buzzer goes off, the opera's not finished until the fat lady sings and the investigation's incomplete till the report's written. This report is the capstone of constant communication between the PI and the client; it is not the only time the PI informs the client what is going on.

In PI fiction, after the initial contact, the only other time the detective seems to see the client is the final scene or if the detective needs to ask more questions or double-check the client's information. In reality, successful PIs do a lot of handholding. People who come to them are usually emotionally wrung out and need constant support. The longer the case, the more the PI must strive to keep the client apprised of what's happening.

As a rule, larger firms tend to provide more and longer reports; some even hand out initial, preliminary and full versions, as well as make repeated reassuring phone calls to clients. Small-town, one-person ops, on the other hand, do most of their "reports" to the client orally. The small agency (especially one without secretarial help) simply cannot afford the time or energy to compile progress reports during the investigation. John finds that the oral report is sufficient to keep the client informed on the disposition of the case while allowing the detective to assure the client emotionally and gather any new or missed information. Still, John does present his clients with a final written report (for a sample, see the Appendix).

In short, all the investigative work—the interviews, the physical evidence, the long hours of driving, the ruses—is useless unless the PI can communicate a condensed version of the experience to the client. Professionalism, then, demands one other skill, the ability to write well. Since the final report is often the detective's last contact with the client, it helps to form that client's lasting opinion of the investigation. Thus, the report also has PR value, and it's no coincidence that it's usually presented with the final bill. John stresses that not only what but how the PI communicates in the report is important. Thus, he believes his English minor gives him a leg up on some other legmen.

Goals

The purposes of the report are often expressed in the acronym TACTICS. Here are the report's seven essential traits.

Truth. Objective details are separated from assumptions and opinions. The complete truth is the ultimate goal of any investigation, though it is rarely attained.

Accuracy. The details are precise as to time, place and people involved. Cross-referencing and corroboration establish the validity of the information. Quotations (exact words) should be documented either through transcripts, notes or references to tapes. A clear distinction is made between objective detail, other information and the PI's conclusions.

Clarity. Detectives assume an audience of functional illiterates (which with John is sometimes the case) or children. PIs use simple language, devoid of big words, jargon and ambiguity. John would never admit it, but right next to his *Hardy Boys Detective Handbook* is Strunk & White's *Elements of Style*.

Thoroughness. The report must make obvious that no stone has been left unturned, no thread not followed to its source. Unfavorable as well as favorable information is provided. John may tone down descriptions of violence, sex and death, but he feels the necessity to include that information. Detectives assume that prior to their reports their clients know nothing, so the report must be complete enough to provide the total picture.

Information. Precise and thorough data is provided. Sufficient specific detail is supplied to justify general conclusions.

Conciseness. Superfluous material is omitted. Long investigations are boiled down to their essence. There is no rambling; every word counts. The reader does not wish to relive the entire investigative experience.

Structure. Reports follow a pattern of introduction, body and conclusion. Transitions should occur between sentences, paragraphs and sections. A thesis governs the report.

Structure of the Report

The final report is written from all the documentation the detective has at hand—notes, earlier reports, physical evidence, records, interviews. The report, as good journalism classes stress, tries to provide the answer to six interrelated questions—who (did it happen to), what (happened), when (did it happen), where (did it happen), how (did it happen) and why (did it happen).

John emphasizes that there is no universal report format, no required length, or even detective style manual. Often the scope of the case and the nature of the client determine how the report is written, the language used and the amount/complexity of detail. For a lawyer, for instance, John writes a digested version of the investigation—meat and potatoes. For a mid-level corporate executive, John will throw in every detail and nuance he can find so as to make the executive look good to his/her superiors—meat, potatoes, vegetables and a little garnish. For a less-educated, noncorporate client, John will often reduce the report to a few choice pieces of meat. John notes that some PIs fashion reports to make themselves look good, and their unofficial rule of thumb is "The more unsuccessful the case, the longer the report."

John believes the best way to write a report is to think of it as a personal letter to the client. He usually begins, "Dear X, My investigation reveals . . . ." At the end he sticks in his conclusions and signs his name. Every report he has ever written breaks down into several components:

1. Title Page
2. Introduction
3. Body
4. Conclusion
5. List of Supplemental Data.

The *title page*, what the client sees first, begins with some sort of letterhead/heading of the detective agency. Below it sits the date, the name of the client, the client's address and phone number, a goal-driven precis of the case and its type (e.g., "To investigate the disappearance of Nora Helmers"), the period the investigation covers (e.g., "New Year's Day through Halloween") and some case name.

The *introduction* provides a sort of thesis/hypothesis that describes the circumstances of the investigation (e.g., "On January 1, 19—, I was retained by Dr. Rank to look into the disappearance of one of his patients, Nora Helmers, who right after Christmas slammed the door on her husband, three children and housekeeper, then disappeared"). An outline statement suggests the major movements of the investigation, highlighting the key evidence.

The *body*, which comprises about 80 percent of the report, offers a chronological summary of the investigation. Each paragraph describes a separate step along the trail (e.g., "At the San Francisco City Courthouse I found incorporation papers for Madame Nora's Doll House . . ."). Logical transitions relate each section. Each paragraph answers the six questions (5W + 1H), giving full names including aliases (e.g. Nora Helmers, aka Madame Nora, aka The Little Squirrel), key dates, complete addresses, the investigator's name (some PIs are unscrupulous enough to list phony operatives to make their agency seem more impressive), evidence uncovered and revelations (e.g., "Kristine Linde, Ms. Helmer's former best friend, stated that the subject wrote three years after leaving Norway, begging her, 'Please come to Frisco in the summer . . .' "). The writing should be simple and clear so the client can easily follow.

The *conclusion*, the final section of the report, contains two separate and distinct portions. The first part is a summary of the information gathered. The second part is the detective's conclusions, opinions and possibly recommendations. For attorneys, John tries to stress the reliability of interviewees, their potential effectiveness in trials, the validity of the evidence collected and the chain by which that evidence was collected. John rarely recommends follow-ups because he cannot rest until he has exhausted all leads and brought the case to a conclusion (e.g., "Madame Nora is quite satisfied with her position and is not likely to return to her husband, Torvald").

The *list of supplemental data* is an inventory of all information collected and available. It contains all the physical evidence, interviews (noting whether they exist in transcript or tape format), any records located (and copied) and photographs.

Other Considerations

- Both the PI's reports and notes are subject to subpoena in civil cases. Accuracy and clarity therefore become important. Opponents often seek out ambiguities in the report on which to build cases.
- All those lessons in English classes are important. PIs, like other professionals, *are* judged by their neatness, grammar, spelling, logic and word choice. Thankfully new computer programs with spellcheck, grammar guide and a thesaurus are available.
- The report must be typed.
- Filing is also important. John worries about break-ins, so every report is filed under a fictitious name that makes sense only to him. He tends to favor names from old movie serials and literature. Ed Hino leaves everything on computer disks. Marilyn Greene keeps boxes in her basement.
- Length. It's relative, depending upon the nature of the case, the extent of the investigation, the education/interest of the client and the fee involved.

Billing

John often hand-delivers the final report. He does so not only to personalize the investigation, but also for pecuniary reasons — it helps him collect his fee. John's bill is complex and differs with every case (see sample bill next page). Generally he has accepted a retainer to start with; against that, he presents documented itemization, including (as mentioned in chapter eleven):

1. any pre-agreed-upon basic fee (he often asks for a "good-faith fee" to look into the case to determine if continuing is possible)

2. per-diems ($XXX/day times number of days; inclusive dates listed)

3. expenses (e.g., mileage, out-of-town fees, rentals, record-locating/copying charges, phone calls, lab fees, hired help/subs, bribes)

4. "hazardous duty pay" (e.g., blackmail negotiations, childnapping exchanges, dangerous areas, known felons).

What happens if the client doesn't pay? As we suggested earlier, John has ways of getting his money (e.g., loss of client confidentiality, the depositing of money in the bank account ruse). Sometimes he is paid in barter (a popular currency in Appalachia); he has received guns, "tobaccy," livestock, even Salvador Dali woodcuts.

Summary

As a writer, you don't need to spend a boring, anti-climactic chapter describing your PI alternately hunched over a typewriter and calculator. However, PIs are businesspersons, and you shouldn't blindly follow the PI fiction cliché that the detective rarely gets paid or that money means nothing. On the other hand, such a cliché might explain why so many detectives work out of seedy offices and drink only cheap liquor—they never get paid. The solution is to have your PI conscious of the impending bill and reports, maybe even occasionally jotting down a few expenses/notes.

Hints

1. Experts estimate that on the average, middle to upper management types spend 50 percent of their time writing. John doesn't think that figure accurately reflects his efforts, but he does have this constant feeling of sitting—before a steering wheel, an interviewee and a computer.

John Landreth
Criminal and Missing Persons Investigations
(606)623-8449

Dear Jack,

The following is an approximate breakdown of expenses encountered in our recent endeavour on your behalf. They are not exact in many respects and I am sure you can understand the impossibility of maintaining exact receipts, records, etc. in the field, under the conditions imposed upon us, by the nature of both our profession and your particular problem. And, of course, this is especially true in a resort area.

Airfare	$456
Airfare (second trip)	468
Automobile, rental and gasoline expense first trip	387
Car rental second trip	591
Hotel, first trip	385
Hotel second trip	260
Food and beverage	339
??? mystery item ???	300
Long distance telephone expense	187
Photography expense (tape, film, special rush developing, equipment rental), etc.	203
Professional assistance	1,430
Miscellaneous expense, airport parking, flowers, gifts for John, court papers, bribes, tolls, etc.	268
Total	$5,274
Expense retainer advance	5,000
Expense balance due	274

As to our fee in the abovementioned matter, we spent a total of twenty complete days on your case, the bulk of which were on the road. The remainder were spent planning, arranging, briefing, getting photos developed, and, of course, finally confronting your daughter. I might add, not included in the above figures are the numerous meetings, phone consultations and conferences with you, of which you will remember only too well. Our per diem for a successful conclusion to a case occurring outside our sphere of influence, such as yours, is $300 a day, which of course, would be $6,000. However, we have decided to accept $5,750 for our fee in the matter.

Very truly yours,

John Landreth

2. Despite the cliché of the detective doing extensive pro bono work, John finds it rarely happens. However, he does engage in some "freebies," though the cases don't always start out that way. It's not so much a general social conscience on his part, but that he runs into some clients who can't afford to pay, yet their needs are important. One time a grandmother asked him to go cross-country to find her granddaughter, but he was already being paid by a bail bondsman to find and arrest the girl's boyfriend. When he delivered the girl to her, the grandmother wrote him a check, asking him not to cash it until the next Monday after her welfare check came in. As John drove away from the hovel, he tore up her check.

3. Sometimes PIs do get paid, but not enough. For an attorney, John once ran a quick background check on a subject for $100. Inadvertently John discovered the man was a heroin supplier. He got subpoenaed for three subsequent complete criminal trials and was paid for none of them. As a government witness, John did receive 22 cents a mile, which amounted to eleven dollars.

N I N E T E E N

THE LAW

If writing a report was the ninth circle of hell, somewhere close to the center right between the fire and brimstone was the courtroom appearance. I sat in my office staring at the perfectly typed subpoena from Phil Landers's lawyer. I wanted to burn the piece of paper, but I was sure it'd give off toxic fumes.

Richard Steele,
Josh Shepherd, PI

Maybe because so many detectives carry badges, writers of PI fiction often portray their protagonists as duly deputized law enforcement agents, characters who work hand in hand with the authorities to bring perps to justice. An equally absurd stereotype is Supertec. Sometimes known as Mike Hammer or Spenser, Supertec operates above the law, breaking into bad guys' offices, committing assault and battery to obtain desired information/confessions and occasionally blowing away particularly evil villains; all the while the authorities turn their heads.

The truth is that PIs are only private citizens. They have not been empowered with any legal rights or privileges past those of ordinary persons. In fact, because of the very nature of their business and because so many investigations end up in court, PIs need a greater consciousness of legal boundaries and restrictions than the average citizen. Everything PIs do, then, from setting up shop to purchasing a firearm, must be in accordance with federal law, state statutes and local ordinances. This chapter provides a review, an elaboration and new information about those times when the PI and the blind lady bump noses.

Licensing. The key is the statutes that establish regulations on the PI industry in that state. Such statutes also describe regulatory overseers, bonding fees, etc.

Firearms. Federal, state and local laws determine what the PI can carry and where. In most states this provision is tied to licensing regulations, thus determining the class of license the PI carries.

Attorneys. Usually they are necessary to help PIs set up shop (e.g., rental agreements), occasionally helping the detective to incorporate (the major advantage is limited liability, which means protecting one's assets; the chief disadvantage, the PI must maintain at least the illusion of a corporation). Many PIs are on retainers to attorneys, performing such tasks as background checks of people and businesses (that truthfully an attorney or an attorney's paralegal could perform).

Search. Some states forbid searches by PIs. Still, it is legal for the detective to search a person's premises if consent is given (or implied). PIs can't obtain search warrants; they can go through the defense attorney who employs them to secure permission. Sometimes the attorney must file a motion for discovery. Sometimes the police fight this motion in court. Some counties — including the one we live in — have open discovery wherein neither forms nor a court order is necessary; PIs who can prove they are working for the attorney of record are given the relevant information.

Evidence uncovered in an illegal search might make good leverage. If a PI does not make a habit of it and has not been established as an agent of the police, a PI could break into a private residence and give found information to the authorities. In fact, the Supreme Court's decision in Burdeau v. McDowell sanctions the seizure of incriminating evidence by private citizens.

Arrest. PIs, like ordinary citizens, may make an arrest. However, they can only arrest on a felony after the crime has been committed, not in anticipation of it occurring. If they arrest a suspect on mere suspicion or somebody else's word, they leave themselves open for 1) charges of false arrest and 2) civil suits.

Specializations. Detectives engaged in divorce cases, for instance, must know the laws applicable in that state. Such things as grounds and custody vary so much. Even to be a process server, the PI must be competent in the relevant law.

Bounty Hunting. Years ago the federal government passed a law allowing private citizens to track down, apprehend and use reasonable force to return fugitives from the law if the citizen is working as an agent of a bail bondsman. Faces on post office walls are fair game for everyone. In John's early years, he supplemented his income by tracing skips. However, as noted in chapter four, this practice is drying up as some states have outlawed private bailbonding.

Contracts With Clients. While John prefers a simple letter of agreement, many agencies, especially large security firms, have legal sections that produce multipage documents.

Accessing Records. A PI has no extra-legal rights to private records. Whatever is available to the general public, the detective can see and copy. Privacy laws shield the remainder. Of course, this legal barrier does not stop a good PI, says John, who, among other things, has learned to take advantage of the new open access laws.

Use of Force. A PI, like any citizen, may use reasonable force in the rare instances 1) when threatened or 2) when others in his/her purview are threatened. That force must be appropriate to the degree of the threat. Physical force must be met with physical, not deadly, force. If a PI is hired to protect private property, for instance, and somebody trespasses, fatal force is not a justifiable response. Detectives who escalate a confrontation make themselves liable for civil and criminal prosecution (some states such as Kentucky allow PIs and all citizens to use any degree of force to defend their homes).

Recording. In most circumstances detectives can legally tape a conversation in which they are one party. Taping an eavesdropped conversation may be illegal and may be inadmissible in court. Some courts have ruled that people who converse in a normal voice in a public place have no reasonable expectation of privacy. PIs, unlike the various levels of law enforcement, cannot obtain court orders for a wiretap. Wiretapping (electronically monitoring a phone) is illegal. The Fourth Amendment does not provide a PI exemption. Conclusion? Wiretapping is illegal and very, very common.

Character Defamation. A PI must verify all evidence. Since a PI's report can be subpoenaed, the detective must be careful in the conclusions of a report not to provide anything that cannot be proven. PIs can be sued in civil courts.

Chain of Evidence. The PI must maintain meticulous records of all evidence—from where it was found to where it went on its way to court. If the evidence is to be used in court, its security must be maintained at all times.

Court Appearances. Only a small portion of John's cases actually come to court. John usually finds himself before a judge in two different roles. In criminal cases he often works for the defense. As an expert witness in weapons, he is also called on to testify. Sometimes he must testify as to photos he has taken or found.

Subpoena. Like any private citizen, John and his records can be required in court, sometimes before a grand jury. For this reason John does not store his notes. He takes them, but he doesn't keep them. If they are subpoenaed, he can truthfully say he has discarded them.

Dial-A-Lawyer

Got a legal problem that's proved an impasse in your latest plot? You can get instant local advice about most problems by calling 1-900-TELELAW. The Huntington Beach, California, firm that answers has a dozen or so lawyers ready to try to answer your question for about $3 a minute. That could work out to $180/hour, which is expensive. The other problem is complex questions.

Worried about being taken? A new federal law provides that 900 numbers charging over $2/call must fully describe their service, then allow you to hang up without being charged should you so desire to terminate the call.

Summary

No matter what your PI's case, you must remember that, despite their frequent proximity to the fringes of the law, PIs are still private citizens. The only differences are that 1) they choose to involve themselves in investigations and 2) they have more expertise in the law enforcement field than Mr. and Mrs. John Q. Public. And of course one of the fiction clichés that happens to be very true is that many PIs are ex-cops.

Hints

1. Just as a real-life PI must constantly consult with attorneys, the writer should be knowledgeable about the law. Maybe like the PI, you can arrange a barter system with local attorneys — they give you a little expertise and you do some writing for them or pick up the dinner check.

2. One way to avoid this interlocking net of laws (federal, state and local) and to maintain verisimilitude is to set your story in a fictitious city and not name the state. Ed McBain places his 87th Precinct series in New Iberia. Still, you should avoid the comic-book sound of Metropolis or Gotham City. A larger problem with fictitious locales is that you must keep exact records of their laws, geography and climates, or you'll have your characters passing a central landmark that is in two different locations.

3. While a PI who constantly quotes the law and the page on which it's found in the civil codes is unbelievable, you do want your detective to have a legal consciousness. If your PI decides to violate a particular law, make him/her aware of doing it as well as its repercussions rather than acting as if s/he's above the law. As to that, John says, "I break the law daily. So does every other PI, bill collector, skip tracer or working policeman. You can't avoid it and still accomplish anything. The laws nowadays are just too mammoth and preclusive. But I am careful to break them only at the minor, minor, minor level. I don't commit felonies — at least not if I can help it."

4. Free legal advice can be found. Try contacting your local bar association (ask any local lawyer for the address) to see if lawyers have previously helped writers, if they operate a legal hotline, if they sponsor a Law Day or if there are associated groups like Volunteer Lawyers for the Arts available.

T W E N T Y

PERSONAL LIFE

*The Landers case was closed tighter than the lid on a pharaoh's
sarcophagus. I'd just finished making still another bargain with the
Devil. Phil Landers had been laundering money for Mr. Euripedes,
who'd sent his button man Louis Vee to keep me off Phil's sacroiliac.
I'd promised to stay away from Phil and had given Mr. E. all the Macon
Whoopee Motel publicity stills. In return, Carolyn had been given a
check with more Zeroes than the Japanese had over Pearl Harbor.*

*So everybody was happy. Carolyn, Mr. E. and me. Especially me in
my seedy office with a bottle of Jack Daniels and a host of silent, drifting
snowflakes to keep me company.*

Richard Steele,
Josh Shepherd, PI

Hemingway thought the best way for the writer to proceed was to
find that one true sentence and then to keep going. John thinks that
the one true sentence that keeps him going through all of Robert
Parker's Spenser books occurs when Spenser tells Susan that he
stays in the PI business because it allows him to live life on his own
terms. But, given that one gift from the gods, John recognizes all
the personal problems a PI encounters because of the nature of
investigative work.

At some time most PIs wonder about a basic chicken-egg problem: Does the detective develop mental problems because of the
nature of the job, or do extant mental problems nudge someone into
the field of private detection? John confesses that's one investigation he's never been able to solve. In any case, all problems are
magnified by on-the-job stress. John believes that the pressures a PI
undergoes are comparable to those of the police, but different in
degree. Cops are caught in a vice between the public and their superiors; PIs deal with fewer members of the public and the majority

have no superiors. Police uniforms single them out in a crowd (many older cops think police blues are like wearing a bull's-eye); PIs have no uniforms and thus are rarely discernible in a crowd on an everyday basis. Police encounter hardened criminals, druggies, drunks and other assorted low-life — people at their worst; with a PI the operative word is choice — PIs determine for whom they wish to work. The police are assigned a beat/case. PIs, then, as Spenser says, have greater control over their lives. Unlike cops, PIs at any stage of their lives or a case can just walk away. This knowledge provides a handy safety valve.

John knows PIs who have dropped out of the profession because of alcoholism, stress, family difficulties and mental instabilities. Still, others suffering these problems have worked through them and stayed on the job. Once again, because there is no PI clearinghouse, universal organization or definitive study, no valid statistics are available on attrition.

Stress

As John has discovered over the years, the sense of being in control does not preclude stress. His time is not really his own, which has caused a major strain on his personal life. After twenty-two years of marriage, he was recently divorced. As hard as he tried, he simply could not leave his work at the office. He recalls one night long ago when his then-wife was truly excited about a progressive dinner they were part of. Coincidentally, for the better part of two years John had been waiting for a teenage girl to whom he could not legally talk about a murder to become an adult. On the day she turned eighteen, she called John and told him she wanted to speak to him. John missed all seven courses of the dinner because he was sitting in a shack in eastern Kentucky listening to the girl describe the last time she had seen her mother alive. The girl's remembrances later convicted her father of murder and made John a lot of money. But John's wife remembered only that she missed the dinner because he was elsewhere.

John also vividly remembers the night of his oldest son's baptism, an event of real importance to the family. Early that day John met with a new client, who asked him to stake out her husband when it became obvious he was going to meet his mistress. John agreed. Guess when the call came? That night. John started the stakeout, popped into the church at the key moment and ended up with two people disgusted with him—his client and his wife. Now John has custody of his two teenage sons, forcing him to manipulate cases and kids. Recently he had to take his youngest son to the hospital with a 104-degree temperature and stay home with him the next day. That meant reshuffling a lot of appointments.

For years every knock on the door at night and every phone call made John's wife nervous. Once, she arranged a surprise birthday party for him. That night the doorbell rang, and a man who looked like Wally Cox asked if he was "the PI." Stepping outside, John nodded and Wally explained that his life was in danger. John stepped back inside with the man, who then explained that his distraught girlfriend was about to set herself on fire. As Wally began really pouring out his heart, the doorbell rang again. It was a nearly nude belly dancer hired by John's wife as a surprise. She was followed inside by thirty people yelling "Surprise" and carrying a birthday cake with burning candles. On other nights people have shown up on his doorstep looking like strays, claiming, "The police gave us your name and address," "The Baptist church said you might help," or "Lawyer Jones thinks you could aid us." No wonder his wife grew jealous of his job.

Being a larger-than-life figure is a double-edged sword. Ed Hino finds his profession opens some doors, closes others. He gets invited to parties, but he's expected to regale the revelers with stories of derring-do.

Neighbors and friends take advantage of John, too. People sidle up to him at parties and ask for free advice. And for everyone who stands there wide-eyed listening to his stories, someone cold-shoulders him because of his profession. When John walks into a local restaurant, he can tell if he's in or out of favor that week by how many "friends" look down at their salads. He never really knows if people are interested in John the man or pissed at Landreth, PI.

Sex

Perhaps the biggest strain for married PIs is on-the-job sexual temptation. The nature of the job is a contributing factor, for, thanks to the media, private investigation is perceived as a glamorous profession. Moreover, the PI often confronts the opposite sex in an emotional context—their spouse is running around, a child is missing.

John admits to having received many offers from women that were doubtless a product of that particular situation. Women perceive him as a crutch and a sexual surrogate. "You," he says, "are the only floating object to people adrift in a wide sea of emotion." Sometimes in missing-person cases, he will travel with a mother as man and wife as a method of getting the child back. He has been on surveillances with wives who insisted on tagging along to watch their cheating husbands. As hubby and floozy exit the motel, John has been offered a sudden payback. And of course in those days his wife used to watch him drive off with strange women.

Effect on the Family

John's two teenage sons can't help but be affected by others' perceptions of him. One day John stopped at a local service station. After filling up, he sent his youngest inside to pay. There, his son heard one of the charter members of the spit-and-whittle club discussing "that crazy Landreth." Another claimed, "He'll kill you for pocket change." Shaken, the boy retreated to the car. It took a lot of self-control for John not to retaliate. John also worries that because he has been in the business a long time, he has made a lot of enemies. Unlike New York, in a small town neither the PI nor members of the family are invisible. His greatest fear is that some local perp he put away will return with a grudge and strike out against his family.

Other PIs

In *Finder*, Marilyn Greene describes her public life of finding lost kids and her private life of losing her family. Gradually her marriage broke up. She found her son drinking at age thirteen. They began to go to counseling together and she remarried. The only constant throughout Marilyn's life has been her compulsion to locate lost kids because sometimes at night she hears them crying.

Gil Lewis, a private eye in Wollaston, Massachusetts, has had only one vacation in twenty years in the field. He works till midnight most nights and doesn't take holidays off. Perhaps his work habits are part of the reason that he is divorced, hasn't kept in touch with his three grown children and lives alone with a dog named Mr. Moto.

Even unmarried PIs have a difficult social life. Dates must be broken because something suddenly comes up. And how would you feel if you were out for dinner with a PI and a strange man strolled up to your table, began cursing and threatening and then reached inside his coat pocket? Or, your date seems strangely preoccupied, a beeper goes off, and there in your date's briefcase you spot a .44 Magnum? Before he was married, and after his marriage ended, John found that because of his job, getting a date was easy; building a relationship was hard.

Alcohol

While some PIs are heavy imbibers, John thinks that drinking on the job is a real taboo. The detective's life might depend on being clear-headed; at the very least performing a successful investigation necessitates making lucid decisions. As previously mentioned, when John finds himself in a bar or lounge (an often-visited locale in domestic as well as criminal cases), he usually orders ginger ale or Sprite — sometimes tea in a shot glass. He wants to blend in with the scene, not become part of it.

John also believes the PI fiction cliché of the detective hanging out at a bar is misleading. Since he does so much work in this particular setting, he is careful not to spend his off-duty hours in such places. He doesn't want to become known in the surroundings. In a big-city environment, obviously this would not be such a problem. John also points out that he doesn't want to associate with the barflies that frequent such establishments. John himself has a two-drink limit at all times and hasn't been drunk in twenty years.

Summary

Ed Hino says that his detective work has had almost no effect on his personal life. Sure, he's missed a tee-time or been late to take out his wife, Marlene, but nothing major. Of course, he admits he's 1) an empty-nester with his three kids having grown up and left home and 2) a part-timer with a full-time profession as well as FBI retirement benefits to fall back on.

Pressure builds some diamonds and crushes other carbon forms. But again, because of the nature of the profession, stats on PI divorces, alcoholics and mental problems don't exist.

Hints

1. The key is that like the rest of us, the PI has a social life. Too much PI fiction leaves the impression that the detective sprang to life as a detective, that s/he does absolutely nothing that's not connected to a case. Emphasize your PI has a social life, and try to create a tension between the public and private side — between the demands of the profession and the realities of trying to establish a social life. In short, make sure your private eye has a private side.

2. Avoid the opposite extreme. Some PI writers spend more time with the private side of the detective than the public. Readers are looking in detective fiction for people unlike themselves, and it's the detective profession that attracts them to the genre. Readers want an inside glimpse of the PI's world, not a pure soap opera. John says that all too often he buys a paperback PI book only to throw it away because the writer did not really want to write a PI book, but rather a disguised treatise about the effect of modern stress on the copulation habits of bluebloods and dashhounds — things that have little or nothing to do with a PI. Don't romanticize or exaggerate the public-private tension in a private eye; just acknowledge it.

   Sometimes rose-colored glasses work okay. John recalls a paperback about a PI riding on the Concorde through a time warp into Christmas Eve, New England, 1850. The book was fair, but the hero could have been any man in any profession.

T W E N T Y - O N E
THE MYERS CASE

By this point, at least one thing should be clear—Josh Shepherd doesn't prowl the same mean streets as John Landreth. But the glimpses you have had into the everyday worlds of John Landreth, Marilyn Greene, Ed Hino and others have at best been fragmented. You've picked up bits and pieces of how actual detectives obtain their licenses, get cases, conduct interviews and gather evidence. What you have yet to see is what a real-life investigation is like from start to finish. To truly understand a PI's work, you need to follow the twists and turns of one particular case, observing what procedures are used, what choices must be made and what connections are spotted. And, to keep the case from being as cold and analytical as those in law school textbooks, you need to know what John was thinking and feeling throughout the investigation.

The Myth of the Typical Case

A caveat: You don't need Marlin Perkins to tell you that there is no such animal as the unicorn, the cameleopard—or the typical case.

Each investigation has a certain uniqueness to it – a sense of something old, something new. And since each PI/firm eventually tends to specialize, what's representative for one detective is idiosyncratic for another. Sure, all detectives have a certain M.O. they like to follow when they get a "wandering daughter job," but throughout the case the detective is going to come to a great many roads diverging in the yellow wood and, based on experience and intuition, decide which path to take.

More caveats – unlike fiction, not every real-life case gets solved; in fact, sometimes detectives, unable to make any headway quickly, give up almost immediately. Also, in real life, a detective rarely has just one investigation going on at any specific time. PIs try to fit the cases in, working one in a heated rush if the trail gets hot or if they are in the right area to continue the investigation; the others are pushed to the back burner to simmer for a while.

Introduction to the Myers Case

Accident investigation provides a good source of revenue for PIs. Sometimes they work for the insurance companies whose parties were involved; other times they are hired by somebody directly or indirectly involved in the accident. Accident investigation is not John's specialty, but the Myers case, which involved the death of a retired autoworker, illustrates the pattern of a PI's investigation as well as the practical use of some of the techniques previously discussed in this book. In addition, John kept meticulous records, including documents and photographs, that can be used to detail his investigation. While the Myers Case actually happened, the names, as *Dragnet* used to remind us, have been changed to protect the innocent – as well as everybody else involved. Even years later, John insists on maintaining client confidentiality.

First Contact

Early one Friday afternoon in the late summer of 1987, John, then married, sat in his living room-office at the desk that doubled as a worktop for him and a sewing machine cabinet for his wife. He should have been working one of the four cases he had on-going at that time, but instead he was preoccupied with the *Smithsonian* magazine that had come in the noon mail. Over the drone of a pair of outside lawn mowers, he heard the phone ring. A law firm in York, Kentucky, for whom he had conducted nearly a dozen investigations wanted to talk with him.

Mostly just to get out of town on a hot, muggy day, John decided to go right then. He drove forty-five miles south on I-75. Hershey, Elway and Amato owned a suite of plush, mahogany-panelled offices in the small town. Senior partner Dick Hershey, a heavy-set man almost as big as his reputation, explained to John that they had recently filed a suit for the widow of a Crenshaw, Kentucky, man who had been killed in a nearby traffic accident. Back on July 1, 1985, Tom Myers had been driving along a rural road when his pickup had been struck, causing it to swerve across the road and come to rest on the shoulder. Myers had died instantly. The other vehicle, a loaded cinderblock carrier, was driven by a man named Davey White who claimed that Myers had in actuality struck him, dislodging some blocks that crashed into the side of Myers's truck. Davey White further insisted that from his vantage point in the cab he had observed Myers reading a newspaper or magazine just prior to the fatal impact.

John's assignment? The firm's case suffered from a lack of documentation. White was the main witness. The accident had occurred in a rural area, so the investigating body was the State Police, who had arrived on the scene some forty-five minutes after the accident; in fact, by the time the trooper showed up, a substitute driver had taken the block truck away. Thus, the trooper's report was vague and very general. If the widow were to be successful in her suit against the block company and its insurance carrier, John would have to locate some witness/evidence that proved Myers was not the one at fault.

Client Assessment

A lot passed through John's mind while he listened to Hershey. With so much time elapsed since the accident, the job would be difficult. And the search for such documentation held only the promise of tedium. Was the usual hourly rate plus per diem worth it?

A second problem was that the accident had occurred in Clement County, Kentucky, and the case would be tried there. From experience John knew the widow's chances of winning were a long shot. A lot of Clement Countians, one of the poorest areas in the country, eked out a living driving trucks; they and their relatives were the ones who would serve on the jury. And even if she won, John was pretty sure the largest jury award in the county had been for $11,000, and that was to a family whose eleven-year-old daughter had gotten off a school bus and was hit by a semi driven by a drunk. At this point, though, the contingency fee was the lawyer's problem. With potentially so little money involved, John knew his chances of a bonus for a job well done were minimal.

John studied Dick Hershey, for whom John had previously located and interviewed witnesses, and even tracked down a witness to an accident who had inadvertently given the police someone else's business card. Hershey, Elway and Amato was a reputable firm that, if not on the side of the angels, at least avoided devils. They had paid all their bills promptly and in full, and they had offered him a $500 retainer. When that was gone, John knew he'd have no trouble requesting more money.

John is essentially a mercenary. If he took the case, he would take it for the money, and he would believe the person in the right was the person paying him. If he uncovered any facts that hindered Hershey's case, he'd point them out to Hershey and try to hide them from the other side.

Though he doesn't talk about it much, John often finds himself siding with the underdog. Had he known then what he later learned — that the block company was conspiring with the insurance company to hide the large amount of coverage — his decision would have come quicker.

And truthfully at that moment John needed money. His oldest son was in braces.

Taking the Case

While Hershey was still detailing the accident, John made up his mind. He agreed to take widow Myers's case. Because he and Dick Hershey were old friends, John didn't bother signing a contract. He did shake the lawyer's hand, but that was after it passed him a check for $500. As is usually the case in a previously successful business relationship, neither side had to sell itself. Hershey did outline his usual considerations: save all receipts and keep a log of all expenses (especially mileage).

"What kind of latitude do I have?" John asked before he left.

"I'd love to tell you to do whatever it takes," admitted Hershey, "but we're in this on a contingency basis."

"And right now you don't have squat."

"Make it happen, John."

Those were the words John wanted to hear.

The Investigation

The investigation actually started before John left the lawyer's office. John picked up the file on the Myers accident and gave it a quick read-through. Then he drove back to Richmond, where he reread the file and watched the videotape made of the accident scene long after the fatal wreck. The tape was valuable in that it gave John a sense of the surroundings and a feel for the case that made it real in his mind.

While he was trying to picture the accident, his wife, Amy, and his two boys came home from a shopping trip. Feeling the warmth of the $500 check in his back pocket, John invited his family out for dinner that night. Then, with some time to kill before going out, John pulled the State Police accident report, complete with stills of the scene, from the file. One of his first moves, John decided, would be to interview Trooper Paul Haynes, the State Policeman who had been the original accident investigator. Right then John called the State Police post at York, where he found Haynes about to go on duty. When John explained what he wanted, Haynes agreed to talk early in that night's shift.

Throughout the fifty-five minute trip to Baxter in Clement County, John could hear and see the disappointment of his family when he had told them he'd have to offer a rain check on that meal. Still, he knew from experience that in cases like this he had to strike immediately when the opportunity presented itself; if the cop were willing to talk that night, John didn't hesitate. Things change rapidly in a case, especially people's minds.

Interviewing the Investigating Officer

At 8:30 Trooper Haynes was waiting as promised at the local Dairy Dee. Haynes, while admitting that his memory was a little foggy, cooperated. Because the cop didn't feel comfortable with a tape recorder going, John took notes.

Eleven months after the accident, when John wrote up his report for Hershey's firm, he devoted five single-spaced paragraphs to summarizing the Haynes interview. Some statements in the formal report are almost verbatim from the interview notes (e.g., the estimate of twenty to thirty blocks falling from the truck). Others John reconstructed from memory and subsequent experiences. Interestingly, the one thing that John jotted down at the interview "To Do" – "what went to KSP [Kentucky State Police] crime lab" – is something that never figured in the case. On the other hand, the seemingly trivial detail of the number of blocks Haynes estimated to have fallen from the cinderblock truck turned out to be a key fact. (John would discover that Haynes, whom he thought a good judge, had been wrong; the actual number John later substantiated was closer to 175 blocks.)

Haynes's opinion (that carries no more legal weight than anyone else's) in both the earlier report and the interview was that the blocks from the cinderblock truck had killed Myers (paragraph four). But, of course, if Myers had struck the block truck first as claimed, he had brought about his own death.

Paragraph five of John's formal report provides no data but rather an assessment of how he views Trooper Haynes's potential as a witness in court:

> In our opinion, Haynes is a plus factor for your client's case. He, of course, will make a good witness on the stand. His report indicates a good, thorough on-site investigation. His personal and professional opinions and conclusions favor your case. The fact that he appears to be a reasonable person who treated White with sympathy and consideration is also good because it makes his conclusion as to White's fault appear to be a fair and just judgment rather than just a hardnosed cop's opinion.

John's interview with Haynes that first night of the case concluded with Haynes taking him to the actual site and walking him through the accident as he remembered it. KY 44 was a typical Kentucky two-lane blacktop with a severe bend in it. Studying the road, John realized that a truck's momentum as it rounded the bend would pull it toward the center line. He could find no lasting impact marks, which wasn't unusual since Haynes hadn't seen any such marks when he arrived at the accident scene, but cinderblock fragments still dotted the roadside. That made John recall Trooper

Haynes's remark about the block truck driver admitting that his straps hadn't been tied down (John's report, paragraph four) and the police report that stated the blocks were "not properly tied down."

Contacting the Opposition

With a phone call from Dick Hershey paving the way, John made tracks to the law firm representing the defendant. He was able to see their file, which in general made clear their claim that Tom Myers's pickup had struck the block truck. The file also contained the original State Police photographs taken of the accident, so John had them copied. One picture in particular immediately caught John's eye, a photo of the victim, Tom Myers, taken at the morgue. In a close-up, John could see a glass shard embedded in Myers's cheek.

Investigating the Truck Driver

When he next got around to the case (he was working several at the time), John realized there were two key roads of exploration his investigation would have to undertake: locating witnesses and examining the cinderblock truck driver. John decided to start with Davey White, the driver. First, to dig up some background information on White's record as a truck driver, John took his Social Security number from the State Police report and filed the proper form with the Kentucky Department of Motor Vehicles. This search turned up a prior. The year before the Myers accident, White had been driving for a local lumber company when a tire blew. The truck was totaled, but no other vehicle was involved (see John's report, paragraph seven).

Needing to interview White, John went to the address that had been listed in the opposition law firm's file. White had moved and was obviously no longer working for the block company (so surveillance of the workplace was out). The neighbors weren't sure where he'd gone. Undaunted, John went down to the local post office in Crenshaw and filed a form with the postmaster (remember, under the Freedom of Information Act, explained on page 102, private citizens have a right to know what information is in the P.O.'s "removal book" for one year). For the price of a dollar, John learned that White was still in town.

Immediately John contacted White and set up an interview. "Somehow" White got the impression that John worked for the cinderblock company's insurance carrier. John simply stated that he was employed by "the insurance company" — vagueness about his client is often advantageous. As a result, White spoke fairly openly about the accident even though investigators for that carrier had previously interviewed him. A couple of key points came out of that discussion: 1) White thought only forty blocks fell, 2) aside from the $500,000 insurance required by law, White's truck had a rider for an extra two million in coverage and 3) the insurance company intended to hide this fact from John's side.

When the interview was over, John phoned Dick Hershey about his discovery. Hershey quickly raised the damages claim in the widow Myers's lawsuit.

John also recalled Davey White's two-page statement to the other side's attorney blaming Myers, claiming the front tire and second tire had to be replaced because Myers had struck and ruined them. This statement was included in John's original report, but is not included in the appendix.

Interview With the Mechanic

Since the block company's Mack truck had been driven from the scene after the accident, John decided to talk to the company's chief mechanic about it. The original maintenance supervisor at the time of the accident no longer worked for the block company and had moved, so John settled first upon his successor, Rip LaBelle. John interviewed LaBelle after working hours and away from the truck company so the mechanic would speak more freely.

Once again, somehow in the confusion at the beginning of John's questions, the interviewee believed John worked for the truck company's insurance carrier. John did not lie — once again, he simply referred to "the insurance company."

Investigation of the Block Truck

Because the block company's substitute driver had driven the truck from the accident scene, Trooper Haynes's report had made no mention of it. But LaBelle admitted that the Mack truck in question, when brought back after finally delivering its payload, did not have the impact marks upon it that would have been there had the trucks collided (John's report, paragraph sixteen). LaBelle's new information, of course, contradicted what White had claimed about Myers's pickup striking him. There had been no new front tires installed as claimed by White. None were needed, for they had been neither struck nor damaged.

Investigation of the Block

From his initial trip to the accident site, John knew a lot of block had been scattered about. He also realized that the greater the number of blocks that had fallen, the deadlier the concrete had been, so he became obsessed with finding out how many blocks had actually fallen on Myers and his pickup. The abundance of fragments he found even later at the site suggested more blocks than either Trooper Haynes or White had claimed.

John questioned people at Ben's Garage, located near the accident site, and learned that a lot of block had lain on the side of the road. Eventually, through their gossip, John located a man who had actually built an entire concrete hut out of the abandoned block — some 100 to 200 of them.

The Crenshaw Block Company had conveniently "lost" their original bill of lading. John knew the truck had been driven off on the day of the accident to Baxter Lumber Company, but since some block had been spilled on the highway, the entire load, could not have been delivered. He found both the original invoice and the invoice for replacement blocks of July 13, 1985. He had been right. About 175 blocks had fallen off the truck, a virtual avalanche of concrete pelting Tom Myers that fateful day. And of course the block company could not refute this information because they had agreed to replace this number free to the buyer; in so doing, they had corroborated the number missing.

Other Witnesses

On Trooper Haynes's original report only one other witness had been named. If John had interviewed Peter Wolf, the driver of a coal truck, long before the trial, then the opposition would have had access to John's report and learned Wolf's testimony would favor Myers, so at the request of Dick Hershey, John waited till just before the trial to obtain the interview.

John also located several other witnesses. Lester Small had been traveling on KY 44 at the time of the accident, so John interviewed him on September 11, 1985, at his place of business, a restaurant in Woodhole near the accident site. John's "Memo to File" on Small makes two points clear: Small believed that White had been traveling at speeds close to sixty miles-per-hour (which made the truck's momentum on the curve in question even greater) and he believed the concrete block truck caused Myers's death.

Davis Montgomery and his wife operated a small restaurant near the accident scene, so over a pork loin sandwich John talked to them and showed them photos. As John notes at the end of the interview, the Montgomerys had been at the wreck, but they had not seen it occur. Thus, they could only repeat what they thought and what others had told them.

Expert Testimony

Lester Small's opinion about the speed of the truck and its subsequent role in the accident was only the belief of an amateur, so the law firm sought a professional engineer/consultant in Lexington. The pro, Vincent Clay, examined the concrete block truck, the KSP report, Seals's statement to Myers's insurance agent and the Kentucky Department of Transportation design plans for the curve. Clay also photographed the scene (after the accident, of course) and made some physics calculations on the speed of the vehicles, the force of the falling blocks and the distances involved. His conclusion is clear and in Myers's favor: "In my opinion . . . the pickup did not impact the block truck causing the blocks to fall off, but that the blocks fell off because they were not secured." This, he noted, was a violation of transportation laws.

The Impasse

While he had made some progress, John knew he hadn't given Hershey much except for the raised claim ceiling. John had a lot of circumstantial evidence, the statements of a few witnesses after the fact (Trooper Haynes and Small), a statement but not physical evidence about the Mack truck's status after the accident and an expert's opinion. Against all of this was the word of the cinderblock truck driver. John was aware he sorely lacked hard evidence—a major witness to the accident or some sort of objective proof of what had really happened on July 1, 1985, along a curve on KY 44.

The Breakthrough

John believes that while the guilty might not have to return to the scene of the crime, the detective always does. So early one spring morning in 1986 John found himself once again prowling around the accident scene, retracing his path, wondering if there was anything he had overlooked, hoping to pick up some hard evidence or at least some good vibrations. While there, he noticed an old man wearing a World War II Army topcoat, a tie, a tie bar and toeless shoes, walking alongside KY 44 with a garbage bag. The scavenger looked to be all of ninety years old.

Eying John with suspicion, he said, "What are you a-doin'?"

John explained that months earlier a major truck accident had occurred right on that very spot and he was investigating it. "You see it?" John probed hopefully.

"Know about it."

"But you didn't see it?"

"Got here right after it happened."

"Damn!" John exhaled slowly.

"Ya want to know what happened, y'oughta check out them pictures."

"I've seen them. But the State Policeman got here after it was all over but the shouting."

"Don't mean him," said the scavenger. "The other guy."

Suddenly the scavenger had John's complete attention. "What other guy?"

"Sure could use a smoke."

"I gave it up."

"I didn't."

"Let's take my car down to the store." They climbed in and John started off. "What other guy?" he repeated.

"You know—coroner."

"The coroner took pictures."

"Hell, poked his camera right inta the pickup."

"You sure it was the coroner?"

"He said so."

"Lakes?" said John. "The Clement County guy?"

"No, next county over."

After buying the old man a pack of Pall Malls, John immediately drove over to the Daniels County coroner's and told him what he wanted. The coroner, however, said there had to be a mistake; he hadn't been near KY 44 the day of Myers's death.

At first John kicked himself for believing something the scavenger had said. The old man had probably wanted to feel important — maybe even needed — and so had made up the tale.

As he left the coroner's, John had another thought. Suppose the coroner had been from even farther east? KY 44 continued eastward into Piketon.

John located the Piketon County coroner, who seemed more movie cliché than real. The owner of a funeral parlor, he was eating a pastrami sandwich, drinking an RC and guiding his apprentice in filling a dead woman with embalming fluid. Between bites and warnings not to let the embalming fluid pressure get too high, the coroner said he had been out of town that day, but not in the direction of Baxter. The man in question could have been his "apprentice coroner" in the west end of the county.

Following the county coroner's directions, John drove twenty miles to an old garage that served as a year-round lawn mower fixit shop. Inside, he found Henry Smith, who admitted to being officially a Deputy Coroner.

"I hear you took some pictures of that wreck over in Clement County last year," John said.

"I did."

"Can I see the pictures?"

"You some kind of official?"

John flashed his license. "I work for the insurance company."

"Okay," said the coroner, "but I never developed the film."

So close, John thought. "What did you do with it?"

"Threw it in my desk drawer over there. Reckon it's still there."

The coroner pawed through the top drawer in what John thought was super-slow motion.

"Yep. Here it be," said Henry, holding up the prize.

"You mind if I develop it for you? I'll pay, of course."

"Go ahead. Just bring it back when you're done."

"Oh, I will," John lied reassuringly.

John immediately drove into Clement. It was now late afternoon. He had to get the film developed quickly, but where? He soon located the office of a baby photographer, who was busy. However, in eastern Kentucky the man who offers cash, cash he doesn't have to go home to get, is king. For $50 the photographer dropped what he was doing and developed the entire roll, making one print of each. John looked them over hurriedly. For $50 more the photographer made him a couple of copies of selected photographs.

At 4:00 P.M. John stopped in a country restaurant, ordered chicken-fried steak and placed a call to Dick Hershey. The lawyer was in conference, so his secretary took the number of the pay phone. John was licking the cherry pie off his lips when the phone rang. "You won't believe what I've got in my hand," he told the lawyer.

One photo revealed that some of the straps on the cinderblock truck were broken, some missing. Other pictures were gruesome, displaying cinderblock fragments embedded in Myers's cab, his eyes and his mouth.

"Bring 'em here now," said Hershey gleefully.

The hard evidence was clear. Myers had been in the right, White in the wrong. In fact, Tom Myers had died painfully, his body crushed by a lot of concrete and even greater human neglect.

Pre-Trial Events

Two important events occurred before the trial. First, the law firm, so elated with John's evidence, cut him in on a percentage basis of the jury award. Of course, if the verdict went against Tom Myers's widow, John would pick up only the agreed-upon fees.

Second, because he was to be a witness, the opposition firm, as part of the discovery phase, took a deposition from him. Instead of sending their top gun, however, the firm assigned this interrogation to two associates, a preppy young man and a young woman.

The couple checked out John's record and quickly sized him up as an aging local investigator, typical security guard material. Of course, John's affected eastern Kentucky dialect also steered them in this direction. As a result of their misperception of his abilities, they weren't very exact or inquisitive with their questions.

After some general talk, the man asked, "Mr. Landreth, at the trial, do you plan to show any photos you've taken?"

This was a key point. Neither Dick Hershey nor John wanted to alert the opposition to the existence of Henry Smith's pictures. Accordingly, John answered the question truthfully, but tried to steer them down the wrong path. "How'd you know I was pretty good with a camera?"

"I repeat, do you plan to show any photographs you have taken?"

"No."

"Have you taken any?"

"You mean, relatin' to the accident?"

"Yes."

"No."

They did not go any further along these lines.

The Trial

During the trial Dick Hershey built up his basic case. Using John's evidence about the true number of blocks that had fallen on Tom Myers, he was able to contradict Davey White's testimony about that detail. From that point on, the jury had to wonder what else White might not have gotten right. After all, White should have known how many blocks had been lost. Then Hershey called John to the stand as an investigator in the case.

"Have you any evidence that suggests Davey White's version of the accident may not be accurate?" asked Hershey.

"Yes, I do," responded John. "Some photographs."

"Objection," said the opposition attorney, who pointed to the discovery deposition in which John had said no to the question of pictures.

Dick Hershey pointed out that John had said that he hadn't taken any photographs.

"Have you discovered the existence of photographs of the accident?" prodded Hershey.

"I have."

When the other side again objected, the judge agreed that John had not lied. The other side simply had not gone far enough with their questions, and the photographs were admissible. Both Henry Smith and John established the well-maintained chain of evidence.

The jury needed only to look at the pictures of the block truck with the broken and missing straps and Tom Myers's mutilated face, his teeth capped by concrete, before deciding in favor of Myers's widow.

The Aftermath

The widow Myers received what was then the largest judgment in a case of this type in Clement County.

John got his percentage. It was the single largest amount of money he had ever earned on a case.

It took John four years from the time Dick Hershey called him at home to finally get his check.

An enlarged picture of the block truck with its missing straps hangs today in Dick Hershey's law office.

After the trial the opposition lawyer admitted to John that he knew the case was lost the minute he saw the photographs John had found. The lawyer then asked for John's card. Since the trial, John has worked for that lawyer, too.

Davey White stopped John in the courthouse after the verdict. "I hope you're satisfied," he ranted.

"If you mean that I'm glad that you won't be driving any twenty-ton, eighteen-wheeler with loose cargo and a looser nut behind the wheel, I am."

"You made me unemployable as a trucker."

John smiled, but his gray eyes were flinty, his voice even as he said, "Not as unemployable as you made Tom Myers."

PUTTING IT ALL TOGETHER

Recently John picked up a PI novel in which a Texas-based detective travels to San Diego, locates a runaway father/husband and talks him into returning to Texas. Before the PI (who hates flying) and the dad drive back, the PI calls his client, the worried wife, and lets her know exactly when they'll be there. When the ride is over, the PI arrives to an empty house because the wife and child have gone to an out-of-town track meet. What does the PI do? He leaves the husband at the empty house where he is promptly murdered.

At that moment John decided the paperback could best be used under a dining room table leg. The flaws in the plot were obvious to an experienced PI. In real life, the mother and child would have waited at home no matter what was going on. And, in real life, if for some reason the family were not home waiting, the PI would have stayed with the runaway at the empty house for two good reasons: The man might get cold feet and run again, and there was the matter of collecting the bill.

Implausibility, especially early in a story, often causes the reader to lose interest. The word "detective" comes from a Latin verb meaning "to take the roof off," which suggests "to uncover what is hidden." Effective writers are detectives, too. They take the roof off their protagonist and uncover the hidden motives that have made that character a PI.

The purpose of this book has been to put you inside a detective's skin. We want you to be able to view the public world through those very private eyes. For your detectives to be believable, they can't just drive the proper car, carry the right weapon or file the correct forms. You must sit inside their skulls and think like them all the time. "If I were a PI who'd just brought back a runaway husband, would I trust him to wait at home alone until his family returned?" Not if you're thinking like a practicing detective whose livelihood, reputation and sometimes even life depends on making the right decisions.

Admittedly, all detectives do not operate the same way; they display the same individuality as people in other walks of life. But there are accepted procedures. And there is an M.O. each detective uses that has evolved from his/her personality. For instance, because John loves kids and has a strong sense of family, he naturally gravitates toward lost child and child custody cases. Another detective with a background in mathematics might specialize in white-collar computer fraud. A detective who has had extensive experience with guns (in the military perhaps) might legitimately choose to no longer carry a weapon and to refuse cases that would probably put him in harm's way (e.g., skip-tracing, repo work, bodyguarding or bounty hunting).

By knowing the PI's boundaries—the uses of research, technical expertise, techniques of surveillance, locating records—you can create an internal consistency in your detective. Should you start writing, however, without considering many of these matters, you leave yourself open for errors in fact and procedure—i.e., plot improbabilities. Sure, some of the time if you make an error (e.g., getting the caliber of a pistol wrong), you might turn off only a small segment of your audience. But if you can get it right, why not? Besides, a slipshod attitude toward one area of expertise can lead to the same less-than-knowledgeable attitude toward other areas. And, given the harsh realities of today's fiction marketplace, you are competing with lots of other writers and would-be writers. Getting it right is one sure way of turning the odds in your favor.

A P P E N D I X

THE MYERS CASE

John's report to Dick Hershey following the conclusion of the Myers case is presented here to give insight into the depth of the investigation. The report contains personal observations, as well as observations of witnesses and officials who were involved with investigating the accident.

Other information that would normally be contained in a final report includes:

- Actual transcripts of interviews or, in their absence, a report of an interview.
- Receipts verifying data pertinent to the case, as well as receipts used to support expense claims for the investigation.
- Letters and reports from "expert" witnesses called in to offer an opinion on a certain aspect of the case.
- Copies of requests filed with other agencies, such as the U.S. Postal Service, to obtain information pertinent to the case.

John Landreth
Criminal and Missing Persons Investigations

709 West Main Street   (606)623-8449
Richmond, Kentucky

June 21, 1986

In reference to the Tom Myers fatal accident that occurred July 1, 1985, my investigation reveals the following:

1. Kentucky State Trooper Paul Haynes, Identification Number XXXX, states that the truck driven by Davey White, which belongs to Crenshaw Block Company had been moved from the scene before he, the police, arrived. Haynes estimates that at least twenty to thirty blocks had fallen off of the truck. He relates that White told him at the scene that Myers was close to the center line but would never say that Myers actually crossed over into White's lane. He also says that Davey White stated to him that he knew before the accident that the blocks were not tied down properly. He further says that White made some statement to the effect that the company did not have enough straps. Trooper Haynes thought most of the fallen block was on the Myers side of the road but not completely off the road onto the right-of-way.

2. Trooper Haynes also makes an observation that we think is very important. He states that he could find no impact mark or sign of one at the scene. Usually when two vehicles collide in any way, dirt (from under fenders, etc.) and debris fall onto the road, making a visible spot that marks clearly the point of impact between the two vehicles. He says that he looked diligently for one but could not locate one at the scene of this accident. He also concedes that this is unusual.

3. Finally, Trooper Haynes says that in his opinion the main cause of the accident was the falling block. It was obvious to us that the trooper believed White's truck was at fault and that the real cause of the accident was the block falling onto Myers. He doubts that Myers hit the block truck before the block fell. But, of course, he could not say so beyond all doubt. However, if questioned in regard to the fatal effects of the accident, he will state that regardless of who was over the line or who hit whom first, in all probability

the accident would have been a minor one, certainly unlikely to cause a fatality, except for the advent of the block's having not been properly secured. I might add that he is quite firm about the block being restrained inadequately. He is definite that it was improperly held in place. He says that it is now his policy to issue citations to trucks that he observes in a similar condition to White's. He does, however, say that at the time he was not inclined to charge White because it was evident that White was upset and distressed over the death of Myers and that he (Haynes) was satisfied that it was an accident. Further, White showed no signs of drinking or other substance use.

4. In our opinion, Haynes is a plus factor for your client's case. He, of course, will make a good witness on the stand. His report indicates a good, thorough on-site investigation. His personal and professional opinions and conclusions favor your case. The fact that he appears to be a reasonable person who treated White with sympathy and consideration is also good because it makes his conclusion as to White's fault appear to be a fair and just judgment rather than just a hardnosed cop's opinion.

5. I probably should also point out that the sketch drawn by Trooper Haynes on the day of the accident showing the direction of travel, etc., differs significantly from the one drawn for me by White on April 24, particularly as to the striking of White's truck cab. Haynes's sketch shows no impact at all involving the cab of the block truck.

6. Davey White is 34-years-old. He holds a chauffeur's license, which was in force at the time of the accident. His driving record shows a speeding violation for which he was cited in James County on August 2, 1984. Our investigation also reveals a truck wreck in 1979 in which White totaled his employer's truck. At the time he was employed by a lumber company located at Kendall near Ford Hill, which was the location of the abovementioned wreck. This employer says that a front tire blew out, causing the wreck. There were no other vehicles involved.

7. White is a tall, sandy-haired man with a pleasant countenance and soft voice. He is somewhat humble and deferring in his conversation. This tends to lend credibility to his statements. However, in our judgment, he is neither intuitive nor especially sharp. Some care should be taken to prevent him from gaining too much sympathy because of his lack of intellect or education. We have

learned that he has worked for Crenshaw Block Company off and on several times, apparently when he is between other jobs.

8. White's statement contains the following: He says that he was close to the centerline but not over it. However, he does not state that Myers was over the line for sure either. He relates that Myers was looking down at a paper or book reading and only looked up with a look of fear on his face at the last minute as he saw White's truck.

9. White believes he loaded the truck himself. (This is confirmed by Rip LaBelle.) He says he had extra restraining straps along in a toolbox behind the cab but decided not to use them. He had checked the load at Moundville and did not feel that they were necessary. He claims that there was white paint on the corner of the trailer. (Rip LaBelle says this was not true.) He looked up after the wreck and saw the camper top spinning in the road. He says that every tire on the Mack truck's left side was involved except the front one. He estimates 40 blocks came off. He says the load was a normal-size load enroute to Baxter Lumber Company in Clement County and was delivered after the wreck.

10. He relates that a man with a gun on his belt told him to move his truck on down the road, so he complied. Oddly enough, he also says that many people did not realize that he was involved or a driver in the wreck. He states that he felt the Myers truck hit him, but does not mention hearing the wreck. This is strange because usually there is a loud noise if cars hit each other at all. He claims that the fuel tank was damaged by Myers but that he did not notice the damage till later, when he got back to Crenshaw, because it had just been repaired from a wreck that occurred at Corbin a short time before (White was not driving).

11. He says that he and others looked for Mrs. Myers's body for a long time in the underbrush off the roadside because people at the scene said she was always with her husband and he had stopped at a store and bought two cokes. The question is, of course, how could White see and notice Myers reading a paper but not see or know whether or not Myers had a passenger up front? You can see down into a pick-up from a big truck very well if you are looking.

12. Davey admits that he has had four or five speeding tickets since 1980. From my investigation, I suspect that he has been cited several times out of state since the accident while driving for his

current employer, Blanton International, which is located in Grant County at Clabin, Kentucky. (Phone: 555-6509.)

13. He says that the tires were replaced on his truck due to the cuts found on them after the accident. (This was not done until after Davey White had left the employment of the block company, approximately four weeks or so later.) White also discovered a broken pin under the rear axle set of wheels on the trailer. One pin was completely gone when he found it, the other was broken but in place. (This broken pin was removed by one of the insurance investigators. I suspect they may try to spring it on you in court.) He says he found the broken pin two or three days after the wreck. This pin was reportedly replaced by the King Body Shop that same week. But according to the King company records, they did not replace any pins for Crenshaw Block Company during the summer or early fall. Finally, Davey says he left the block company due to getting a better job and was not fired.

14. Rip LaBelle is the mechanic for Crenshaw Block Company. He lives on the quarry site and is apparently also some sort of informal foreman or overseer. He took White to the hospital after the wreck when Davey became emotionally upset and had trouble breathing. He says that he had seen Davey slipping out several times before with his cargo load improperly secured. By "slipping out" he meant getting gone before anyone could say anything to him. La-Belle says that he had been intending to say something to White about it but it kept slipping his mind.

15. He recalls no impacted paint marks on the tires or on the trailer or the tractor showing contact with the Myers truck. When pressed by me, he reluctantly admits that he would have seen them had they been there, but he did not see any paint marks. He says that the gas tank was scratched up but had no paint on it. He believes that the Myers truck might have done damage to it and that is why there were no paint marks: He may have hit it with the chrome part on his rear bumper. LaBelle had just repaired the gas tank and buffed it out from a previous wreck. (I have a photo of the damage to the tank.) Also, he says all of the tires on the outside left side of the truck had cuts which he said looked like "curb burns" (concrete cuts). This includes the front tire which Davey had said was uninvolved in the wreck, yet it also had cuts, according to Rip.

16. LaBelle points out that White was newly married and consequently often in a hurry to get the job done to get home early. He

states that company policy is to tie cargo down with straps placed over angle iron, which is laid on the corners of the top row of blocks.

17. He says he saw no black paint anywhere on the block truck. He agrees that the pin could be broken by a sudden jerk such as a sudden swerve to the right or a yank (a reaction to load drop). He also admits that the pin could have been broken days before the accident and escaped notice. In conclusion, Rip says that if anything was wrong, it was negligence of the driver at the time of the accident. The block company had only two drivers and several extra trucks, so plenty of extra straps were available to Davey.

18. Our opinion of Rip LaBelle is as follows: He is very loyal to Mr. Ed Westly, the owner of the block company. He expressed some fear to us about "getting in a bind" by telling us what he knew. He will consequently be reluctant to testify, but we believe that in light of the taped conversation we have on file he will stand by his earlier statements to us unless specifically ordered to lie by Westly or some agent of the insurance company. He is somewhat sharper than White, although similar in appearance. If not instructed otherwise, he will place blame on Davey White without realizing that this hurts the block company as well. If this occurs, he will make an excellent witness for your side in the case.

19. The truck in question is a late model Mack, 1984 or 1985, blue, and had very low mileage on it at the time of the wreck. After the wreck, it was driven to the job site and unloaded by another driver, Otis Tareyton. The Mack truck is a huge vehicle with a rear tandem that can be moved: wheels can be slid forward and backward and are adjustable by removing a pin. This restraining pin was broken after the wreck and is the one in question.

20. The metal end-clip on the front restraining strap on the left-hand side of the truck was broken off and gone at the time of the accident and consequently would not buckle properly. (The photo shows this clearly.) Both Rip and Davey White say it is still possible to tie the strap in place, but they admit that he did not do this. They say the buckle had been gone for a long time.

21. Mr. Ed Westly, the owner of the block company, was out of town on vacation at the time. He is reportedly very wealthy and one of the most influential men in Crenshaw. Our investigation indicates that the company has a one million dollar override liability policy in addition to the five hundred thousand dollar policy required by federal interstate transportation laws to operate this type

of vehicle. We have learned that, because the policies are separate rather than a combined policy, the underwriters hope you will not learn or discover the full extent of their liability in this matter. In fact, they intend to keep you uninformed if at all possible. I feel sure you will now know how to act accordingly.

22. In conclusion, let me point out that we have also obtained several photographs taken at the time of the wreck that were not part of the official State Police investigation. They, of course, speak for themselves. I still have possession of the negatives, and perhaps we should meet soon to go over all the photos in case you want more copies or enlargements. I, of course, have maintained a strict chain of evidence on these negatives but should return them to their proper owner sometime soon. I also have taped copies of all the interviews, including ones with Tom Kramer, Adam Jones and Davis Montgomery. All of these are people in the Clement area who were at the scene after the accident and whose opinion and observations favor your client's case.

23. There remain several loose ends we would like to nail down in this matter, however. We have been waiting for further instructions regarding these. As I reminded you the other day, Dick Hershey had requested that we hold off on interviewing several people, including Peter Wolf and the Clement County Coronor. We await further instructions from you in these matters. As always, if you have any questions, please do not hesitate to call me.

I remain sincerely
your friend,

John Landreth

Bibliography

Berko, Robert, and Sherry Sadler. *Where to Write for Vital Records of Births, Deaths, Divorces and Marriages*. South Orange: Consumer Education Research Center, 1989.

Beyette, Beverly. "How to Uncover Your Lover." *The Courier Journal*. October 5, 1989: Sec C:1,6.

Blye, Irwin, and Andry Friedberg. *Secrets of a Private Eye*. New York: Henry Holt, 1987.

Brown, Sam, and Gini Scott. *Private Eyes: What Investigators Really Do*. New York: Carol Publishing, 1991.

Buckwalter, Art. *Interviews and Interrogations*. Butterworth's Library of Investigation. Boston: Butterworth, 1983.

— — —*Investigative Methods*. Butterworth's Library of Investigation. Boston: Butterworth, 1984.

— — —*The Search for Evidence*. Butterworth's Library of Investigation. Boston: Butterworth, 1984.

— — —*Surveillance and Undercover in Investigation*. Butterworth's Library of Investigation. Boston: Butterworth, 1983.

Canedy, Dana. "When Others Fail, Marilyn Greene Can Find the Body." *The Wall Street Journal*. August 1987: 1,19.

Cunningham, William, and Todd Taylor. *Private Security and Police in America*. Boston: Butterworth-Heinemann, 1984.

Ferraro, Eugene. *You Can Find Anyone: A Complete Guide on How to Locate Missing Persons*. Santa Ana, California: Marathon, 1988.

Friedman, Jon. "This Gumshoe Does His Legwork in Wing Tips." *Business Week*. May 29, 1989: 98.

Greene, Marilyn, and Gary Provost. *Finder: The True Story of a Private Investigator*. New York: Crown, 1988.

Grover, Ronald, Joseph Weber, and Keith H. Hammonds. "That's Sam Spade Leafing Through the Ledger." *Business Week*. May 29, 1989: 95, 98.

Johnson, Harriet C. "Sleuths Open Eyes of Big Biz." *USA Today*. June 3, 1984: Sec. B-2.

"Just Dial 1-900-CHEATER." *Newsweek*. July 29, 1991: 58.

Lehman, David, and Lynda Wright. "Seeking the Existential Sleuth." *Newsweek*. June 13, 1988: 75.

McCrie, Robert, Ed. *Security Letter Source Book 1990-1991*. New York: Security Letter, 1990.

Millman, Joe. "Spook for Hire." *Forbes*. March 18, 1991: 138.

Morais, Richard. "Sam Spade Goes Corporate." *Forbes*. February 25, 1985: 26, 27, 29.

Nemeth, Charles. *Private Security and the Investigative Process*. Cincinnati: Anderson Publishing Co., 1992.

— — —*Private Security and the Law*. Cincinnati: Anderson Publishing Co., 1989.

Parkhunst, William. *True Detectives: The Real World of Today's PI*. New York: Crown, 1989.

Pileggi, Nicholas. *Blye, Private, Eye*. New York: Pocket Books, 1987.

Revkin, Andrew C. "Organ Hunter." *Discover*. February 1988: 64-69.

Security Industry 1990 Edition. Bethesda: C&P Telephone of Virginia, 1989.

Sedgwick, John. *Night Vision: Confessions of Gil Lewis, Private Eye*. New York: Simon & Shuster, 1982.

Smith, Edward. *Practical Guide for Private Investigators*. Boulder: Paladin Press, 1982.

Thompson, Josiah. *Gumshoe: Reflections in a Private Eye*. Boston: Little, Brown, 1988.

Wilson, Keith. *Cause of Death*. Cincinnati: Writer's Digest, 1992.

Wingate, Anne. *Scene of the Crime*. Cincinnati: Writer's Digest, 1992.

Secondary Bibliography

Akin, R.N. *The Private Investigator's Basic Manual*. Springfield, Illinois: Charles C. Thomas, 1976.

Barefoot, J.K. *Undercover Investigation*. 2nd ed. Woburn, Massachusetts: Butterworth, 1983.

Battle, B.P., and P.B. Weston. *Arson Detection and Investigation*. New York: ARCO, 1978.

Bennett, Georgette. *Crime Warps: The Future of Crime in America*. Garden City, New York: Doubleday, 1987.

Blackwell, G. *The Private Investigator*. Woburn, Massachusetts: Butterworth, 1979.

Block, Eugene. *Famous Detectives*. New York: Doubleday, 1967.

Bozza, C.M. *Criminal Investigation*. Chicago: Nelson-Hall, 1978.

Brady, J. *The Craft of Interviewing*. New York: Vintage Book, 1977.

Carroll, J.R. *Physical and Technical Aspects of Fire and Arson Investigation*. Springfield, Illinois: Charles C. Thomas, 1979.

Conway, J.V.P. *Evidential Documents*. Springfield, Illinois: Charles C. Thomas, 1978.

Cunliffe, F., and P.B. Piazza. *Criminalistics and Scientific Investigation*. Englewood Cliffs, New Jersey: Prentice-Hall, 1980.

Draper, Hilary. *Private Police*. Atlantic Highlands, New Jersey: Humanities Press, 1978.

Eames, Hugh. *Sleuths, Inc.* Philadelphia: J.B. Lippencott, 1978.

Fallis, Greg, and Ruth Greenberg. *Be Your Own Detective*. New York: M. Evans and Company, 1989.

Fuld, Leonard. *Competitor Intelligence: How to Get It, How to Use It*. New York: John Wiley & Sons, 1987.

Given, B.W., R.B. Henrich, and J.C. Shields. *Obtaining Motor Vehicle Evidence From Tire Tracks and Tread Marks: Complete Reference for Collecting, Recording and Analyzing Track and Tread Evidence*. Houston: Gulf Publishing, 1976.

Golec, A.M. *Techniques of Legal Investigation*. Springfield, Illinois: Charles C. Thomas, 1976.

Hayduke, George. *Get Even: The Complete Book of Dirty Tricks*. Boulder: Paladin Press, 1980.

Henderson, M. Allen. *Flim Flam Man: How Con Games Work*. Boulder: Paladin Press, 1985.

Hicks, D.D. II. *Undercover Operations and Persuasion*. Springfield, Illinois: Charles C. Thomas, 1973.

Holt, Patricia. *The Bug in the Martini Olive*. Boston: Little, Brown and Company, 1991.

Hunt, William R. *Front-Page Detective: William J. Burns and the Detective Profession 1880-1930*. Bowling Green: Popular Press, 1990.

Inbau, F.E., and J.E. Reid. *Criminal Interrogation and Confession*. Baltimore: Williams and Wilkins, 1967.

Joseph, A., and H.C. Allison. *Handbook of Crime Scene Investigation*. Boston: Alyn and Bacon, 1980.

Lapin, Lee. *How to Get Anything on Anybody*. Foster City, California: Crocker-Edwards, 1983.

Lilly, G.C. *An Introduction to the Law of Evidence*. St. Paul: West, 1978.

McCartney, Robert J. "Turning a Private Eye on Saddam Hussein: Corporate Sleuth Jules Kroll Hired by Kuwait." *The Washington Post*. March 26, 1991: Sec. C:1.

McGrew, D.R. *Traffic Accident Investigation and Physical Evidence*. Springfield, Illinois: Charles C. Thomas, 1976.

Mettler, G.B. *Criminal Investigation*. Boston: Holbrook Press, 1977.

O'Hara, C.E. *Fundamentals of Criminal Investigation*. Springfield, Illinois: Charles C. Thomas, 1973.

O'Hara, C.E., and J.W. Osterburg. *An Introduction to Criminalistics: The Application of the Physical Sciences to the Detection of Crime*. Bloomington: Indiana University Press, 1972.

Osburn, A.S. *Questioned Documents*. 2nd ed. Montclair, New Jersey: Patterson Smith, 1978.

O'Toole, George. *The Private Sector*. New York: Norton, 1978.

Pearce, William W., and William Hoffer. *Caught in the Act: The True Adventure of a Divorce Detective*. New York: Stein and Day, 1976.

Penofsky, D.J. *Guidelines for Interrogations*. Rochester: Aqueduct Books, 1967.

Pyke, Nicholas. "Playing Hide and Seek in Deadly Earnest." *Times Educational Supplement*. December 28, 1990: 3.

Roblee, C.L., and A.J. McKechnie. *The Investigation of Fires*. Englewood Cliffs, New Jersey: Prentice-Hall, 1981.

Royal, R.F., and S.R. Schutt. *The Gentle Art of Interviewing and Interrogation*. Englewood Cliffs, New Jersey: Prentice-Hall, 1980.

Rush, Donald, and Raymond Siljander. *Fundamentals of Civil and Private Investigation*. Springfield, Illinois: Charles C. Thomas, 1984.

Schultz, D.O. *Crime Scene Investigation*. Englewood Cliffs, New Jersey: Prentice-Hall, 1977.

Scott, C.C. *Photographic Evidence: Preparation and Presentation*. 2nd ed., 3 volumes. St. Paul: West, 1969.

Siljander, R.P. *Applied Police and Fire Photography*. Springfield, Illinois: Charles C. Thomas, 1976.

— — —*Fundamentals of Physical Surveillance: A Guide for Uniformed and Plainclothes Personnel*. Springfield, Illinois: Charles C. Thomas, 1977.

Stewart, C.J., and W.B. Cash, Jr. *Interviewing Principles and Practices*. 3rd ed. Dubuque: William C. Brown, 1978.

Sulner, H.F. *Disputed Documents*. Dobbs Ferry, New York: Decana, 1966.

Thomas, Ralph D. *How to Find Anyone Anywhere: Secret Sources*. Austin, Texas: Thomas Publications, n.d.

Thompson, Leroy. *Dead Clients Don't Pay: The Bodyguard's Manual*. Boulder: Paladin Press, 1984.

Underwood, Doug. "The Pulitzer Prize Winner who Became a Private Eye." *Columbia Journalism Review*. September-October 1989: 41-45.

Wanat, John A., Edward T. Guy, and John J. Merrigan, Jr. *Supervisory Techniques for the Security Professional*. Boston: Butterworth, 1981.

Weston, P.B., and K.M. Wells. *Criminal Investigation Basic Perspectives*. 3rd ed. Englewood Cliffs, New Jersey: Prentice-Hall, 1980.

Young, Johnny. *Vanish: Disappearing Through ID Acquisition*. Boulder: Paladin Press, 1986.

Index